Bonded Vault

Based on the true story of the brazen robbery

of a secret mob vault

David Aiello

Wendy,

I hope you enjoy the

book.

[signature]

Bonded Vault

After planning the heist for several months, eight brazen criminals, on August 14, 1975, robbed the Hudson Furs/Bonded Vault Storage Facility in Providence, Rhode Island. Very few Rhode Island residents, including those in the law enforcement community, knew that the dilapidated, unassuming red brick building was the secret location of 146 large steel-reinforced vaults where mobsters hid millions of dollars of silver, gold, precious gems, and vast amounts of undeclared cash. All other heists of that period, including the multimillion-dollar Lufthansa robbery, pale in comparison to the amount stolen in the Bonded Vault robbery.

The Bonded Vault robbery has become a legend in the annals of mob lore as one of the most bizarre and most profitable robberies of its time.

Some of the names of the participants in the robbery, as well as those in law enforcement investigating the heist, have been changed. Some characterizations are composites. Certain content, situations, and timeframes of events have been altered for dramatic purpose.

Absalom and Achitophel, John Dryden, originally published 1681, lines 83–84.

"The Show Must Go On," Three Dog Night version, lyrics by Leo Sayer
and David Courtney,
Chrysalis Records, copyright 1973.

"The Ballad of Mack the Knife," *The Threepenny Opera*, lyrics by Kurt Weill
and Bertolt Brecht,
copyright 1928.

Cover design by Michael A. Aiello

ISBN: **1547243538**
ISBN 13: **978-1547243532**

Wet Dreams

Lies, deception, misdirection, false narratives, coercion, misinformation, and suspension of disbelief were some of the tools of the trade and tactics used by writers, stockbrokers, corrupt politicians, and Vincent "Jay" Verde, the FBI Director of the Rhode Island's Organized Crime Task Force.

September 24, 1975, had been a mundane day for Jay Verde in the Providence office of the FBI. The average person who watched too many police melodramas on television are given the false impression that most every day, FBI agents were involved in violent gun battles with arch criminals carrying automatic weapons or in pursuit of notorious serial killers. But in the real world of law enforcement, most investigations were boring and methodical. Most of the time, endless leads never produce any results. Sometimes crimes were solved by the agent's cunning, years of experience, reliable informants, or just plain luck.

However, Agent Verde's career had been the exception. He was relentless when perusing a suspect and was considered one of the best FBI profilers and field agents. He had achieved national acclaim and was awarded a special citation by the director of the FBI for the planning and coordination of a multistate joint investigation with the DEA that led to the arrest and conviction of twenty drug traffickers working for Pablo Escobar's Medellin cartel. The sting operation netted five tons of pure uncut cocaine and twenty million in cash.

Agent Verde was usually referred to by his nickname, Jay, or simply called by his last name. His brown hair matched his dark, foreboding eyes. He was overly vain about his bold, chiseled facial features. He was athletically built, standing nearly six foot two, which gave him an imposing and commanding presence.

Verde's agents were currently coordinating a joint investigation with the Providence and state police on the Bonded Vault robbery a secret mob storage facility in Providence. None of the reliable informants or the usual suspects had any solid leads. FBI Agents had conducted interviews with the "vault" holders from the list provided from the storage facility's owner. Many of the people who were robbed had criminal records and were evasive and reluctant to disclose the contents of their lockers. Verde surmised that most of the vaults contained undeclared valuables and that few had even filed insurance claims, fearing that they would be charged with tax evasion.

Earlier in the day, Verde had received a missing-person report over the teletype. At first he didn't give it much thought. After all, cases like those were under the jurisdiction of the local police, and not something the FBI would waste their time investigating. The missing person's name was Ralph Imperatore.

Since it was a slow day, after eating lunch at Angelo's Restaurant on Atwells Avenue, Verde obtained Imperatore's social security from the IRS and ran his identification through the Bureau of Criminal Investigations (BCI) database. Ralph Imperatore did not have a criminal record.

Out of curiosity, he ran the name through the DMV database and a Rhode Island Property Records report.

Verde's curiosity grew as the he read the information. Ralph Imperatore was a twenty-nine-year-old long-term substitute teacher (LTS) at Mount Pleasant High School in Providence. The DMV records indicated that he owned expensive luxury and sports cars, including a Mercedes convertible, a Shelby Cobra GT 500, and a Cadillac Coupe De Ville. The Rhode Island Property Records report showed that he owned several investment properties in Rhode Island and a waterfront house in the Riverside section of East Providence.

Verde knew something was wrong with the profile. It didn't add up. According to the IRS records, he only made approximately 15000 a year since graduating college. He could not have amassed this wealth on the pay of a substitute teacher, Verde thought. He decided that later in the day, he would visit the address the Providence School Department was sending his checks

***

In his moments of solitude, Verde often looked at the old photographs of his family on his desk next to files of ongoing and previous investigations. His father died when he and his brother were young, and his mother did her best to raise her two boys and manage the household expenses.

In a sliver frame was a picture of his brother dressed in a leisure suit when he attended a ceremony in his honor for being inducted into the Rhode Island's Baseball Hall of Fame. He had been a three-time all-state selection for his standout play. As a ninety-four-mile-an-hour left-handed pitcher, he had received scholarship offers by many division-one colleges and had received offers to attend camps showcasing his talent for professional baseball teams. Now, Verde thought, shaking his head, his brother had been inducted into Rhode Island's Hall of Shame. He was a convicted criminal. He received six months probation for running policy slips and sports betting cards for the mob. Seven months later he received two years in the Adult Correctional Institution for receiving and selling stolen goods, bookmaking, and loan sharking. He had it all—talent few possessed, a bright future in sports—but he threw it all away.

Verde's mind digressed. He thought about his humble beginnings and how far he had come. He had learned from the mistakes he made in his past and often took refuge and comfort there. He and his brother were born and grew up in the gutter on the "mean streets" of the Italian neighborhood known as Federal Hill. His mother was insistent that her sons attend Saint Mary's School to receive a proper and Christian education. However, the formal education they received in school was secondary to the lessons they learned, the hard way, on those streets. The curriculum had advanced degrees in ultra-violence and intimidation. Every avenue was their classroom with educational tools like Louisville baseball bats, zip guns, and stilettos. Paranoia and violent acts were as commonplace as going to the corner store for a slice of pizza and a Coke. You learned, or had to learn, at a very early age, to talk the talk, walk the walk, and most important, to stand your ground. If you showed any sign of weakness, the wannabes who were young apprentice gangsters would take advantage of you. You learned, out of self-preservation, by any means necessary, to protect yourself with a lug wrench, a broken beer bottle, or anything else you could pick up to ward off anyone who meant to do you harm. He and his brother graduated from those mean streets, earning their diplomas with high honors.

To an outsider, the lifestyle appeared to be one of degenerates, or at best, in the case of the Verde brothers, educated derelicts. In hindsight, Verde now knew, they were probably right. Most of the "wise guys" and "wannabes" were shortsighted and had misguided priorities, goals, and codes of conduct.

Verde used what he learned on those mean streets to catch the same men he could have easily become, knowing, as the saying goes, "But for the grace of God go I." In retrospect, he would not have changed anything about his childhood, except maybe his brother's past.

***

The criminal empire of the mean streets was controlled with an iron fist by Raymond L. S. Patriarca, who was affectionately known by his close associates as the Old Man.

Everyone living on Federal Hill knew Patriarca was a gangster, a man who was respected and feared. The mob would use those words "respected" and "feared" interchangeably, and when they referred to the former, they usually meant the latter. As Verde was growing up, no one knew, not even those in law enforcement, how powerful and influential the Old Man really was, and his true status in the underworld. That is, not until New York mobster-turned-informant, Joseph Valachi, testified before a televised Senate committee hearing on organized crime and named Patriarca as the head of New England's La Cosa Nostra. After that Senate hearing, the bravado of the mobster's attitudes up the Hill was palpable. All the wise guys walked with a swagger in their step, heads held high with an air of superiority now that everyone knew they were a member of a crime family under the protection of one of the most powerful dons on the East Coast.

The Old Man took his share of bookmaking, illegal gambling, loan sharking, and hijacking, which was referred to as his tribute. He forbade any activity on his turf that would draw too much heat from law enforcement or the local newspapers. He knew that if heinous, high-profile crimes on his turf put his organization in the spotlight, the corrupt politicians and cops on the take would no longer cover up the criminal activities they were being paid so handsomely to overlook. From the beginning of the Bonded Vault investigation, Verde knew that a heist on the Old Man's turf could never happen without his blessing.

During the Old Man's long reign, misguided principles were viewed by many as acceptable ideals to govern their lives, but more important it was an ideology of flawed perspectives.

***

At various locations on the mean streets, the denizens—wise guys, associates, and wannabes—would be hanging out, protecting their own piece of the Hill. As a teenager Verde and his friends admired and wanted to emulate those men. It was an enticing trap—new clothes, wads of money, and homes furnished with all the latest appliances, all of which, they would joke, fell off the back of a truck. In retrospect, he now knew his childhood admiration for those men was misguided.

Most of those criminals had similar ambitions, known as "wet dreams." Some wanted to become members of a crew to pull down scores. Others were waiting for orders to whack someone and "make their bones" and become "made" members of the Mafia, which gave them the right to operate their own crews.

In Verde's youth, his wet dream would come strolling down Atwells Avenue every week day at lunchtime. It was Jennifer Del Marco.

Like clockwork, every day just before noon, a crowd would mysteriously assemble outside the barrooms and restaurants, just waiting for her to pass by. She would come strolling down the avenue wearing a tight-fitting miniskirt, a long gate in her step, gliding her long, tanned, sinewy legs as if she was walking on air. The top of her breasts were always mostly exposed, and her erect nipples protruded through her sheer dress like sewing thimbles. She always liberally applied jasmine perfume, which permeated the avenue in her wake. Jennifer knew the effect she had on the men and craved their attention. Young Verde knew better than to gaze upon her for too long or talk to her. All the wise guys had secret plans that one day she would become their wife, or at least their *gumatta*: a married man's girlfriend. Verde knew that you could easily catch a beating for eyeballing the wrong person or staring at or talking to a coveted beauty like Jennifer.

***

After graduating from college, Verde joined the state police. When he entered the state police training academy, the instructors viewed him with skepticism, and he took a ribbing from some of the other candidates when they found out his brother was a convicted criminal. Verde graduated from the state police academy in the top percentile of his class. Many of his classmates were "bookwise" but not streetwise. Verde guessed that was all right as long as they were merely revenue agents for the state, handing out speeding tickets instead of the elite law enforcement officers they were pretending to be. He came to realize that there were also many brilliant investigators on the force who were as competent as he was and a few even more astute. Due to Verde's diligence and perseverance, in a short time, his fellow officers and superiors regarded him as one of the best on the force.

After ten years as a state police detective, Verde was offered director of Rhode Island's FBI's Organized Crime Task Force. Before accepting the position, he took a sabbatical from law enforcement when Hollywood called. Because of the notoriety he had received in the high-profile cases he had solved, he was offered a temporary position as a consultant on Francis Ford Coppola's mob movie, *The Godfather*. The studio believed who better than Verde—who had walked on both sides of the street, who knew how mobsters spoke and thought and the brutality that the Mafia could exhibit—to give the movie an air of authenticity.

After the movie was finished, two things happened. He became the FBI Director in Rhode Island and drew the ire and hatred of many of those in the state police and the Rhode Island law enforcement community. Some of their animosity was due to Verde's arrogance and part was from jealousy. In any event, from that day forward, his detractors would condescendingly refer to him as Hollywood.

Now a day, he prowled the mean streets he used to roam, driving a black Crown Victoria with a gun and an FBI badge and all the authority it signified. It was no longer him but the wise guys who dared not stare, and when they saw him coming, they looked the other way. He became the most despised alumni on the Hill. He was hated more than any mob informant, any "rat." In their twisted way of thinking, most everyone on Federal Hill believed he had betrayed his heritage, his neighborhood, and his childhood friends.

***

Verde never really knew why his brother had taken the opposite direction in life. He had heard all the lame excuses from all of the men and women he had arrested over the years as to why they took up a life of crime. He and his brother had been nurtured under the same conditions but yet he took the road less traveled while his brother had taken the path of least resistance. He had witnessed the prejudice associated with his Italian heritage when he joined the state police. He never let it affect his fortitude, believing that the true test of a man's character is how he deals with adversity, and in spite of it, or because of it, he succeeds.

The story his brother told him, as an attempt to rationalize the path he took, happened when he was ten years old and his brother was twelve. It had been a cold winter day. The Verde family had just returned from Sunday church services. As their mother and father were preparing their traditional Sunday dinner of macaroni, meatballs, and a pitcher of orange soda spiked with a glass of Pastine red wine, the boys played hide-and-seek in their basement. Ray Verde had hidden in an old, unused coal bin. There was an old metal sign nailed over the old coal shoot to keep out the cold and the rats. The sign read: "Uncas Manufacturing. Help Wanted. Italians need not apply." When they went upstairs for dinner, Ray asked his father what the sign meant. His father tried to downplay the significance of the sign. He did not want his sons to become jaded, and he explained that since that time things had changed. Their father told them that around the time of the Great Depression, people of Italian decent were considered second-class citizens in Rhode Island by the establishment. His father had worked a double shift, and on his way home one night, he ripped the sign off the building, believing it was an insult to his heritage. He told the boys that if that sign had been up after he and the boys on the Hill returned from World War Two, they would have burned the building to the ground out of disrespect.

Ray Verde said he would never follow in his father's footsteps, leading a straight and honest life that led nowhere except to an early death. He felt his father's only reward, in this life anyway, was an early one-way trip in the back of a black limousine. Years later, Verde told his brother his rational was bullshit and showed him no empathy.

***

Later that afternoon, Verde went to Prudence Avenue in the Silver Lake section of Providence. That was the address the Providence School Department had been sending Ralph Imperatore's checks .

The small, white vinyl-sided bungalow-style house was well kept. In front of the house was a makeshift grotto made with a vertical half-buried old bathtub painted sky blue with a white cement statue of the Madonna in the middle. An elderly woman answered the door. She told Verde she was Imperatore's grandmother. He told her he was with the FBI, assisting the Providence Police on the missing person's report of her grandson. She spoke softly in broken English.

The woman reminded Verde of his own grandmother. She was barely five feet tall and three feet wide, wearing a floral housedress and a white apron that nearly touched the old linoleum floor. There was a pot of gravy simmering on a white porcelain gas stove. She had been peeling vegetables for the lentil soup she was making. The walls of the outdated kitchen were adorned with pictures of various saints and small religious statues in alcoves and niches. She told Verde that her Ralphie was a good boy, a straight-*A* student who took her to church every Sunday and was never in trouble with the law.

"My son died when Ralphie was young," she said. "His mother abandoned him and lives in Scottsdale, Arizona. I don't talk to her. I raised Ralphie like my own son," she said, making a small sign of the cross.

She took out a small metal box and showed Verde her grandson's baptism and confirmation certificates.

"I see you have a few photographs of your grandson," Verde said. "May I have one…for the investigation?"

"Sure. He's a good-looking man, tall, well built, and handsome, just like you," she said, with a half smile.

Her tiny hands were trembling as she handed him a recent photograph. "I reported Ralphie missing after the principal at the school said he didn't show up for work in three days. That's not like my Ralphie. He a good boy. Takes me to church every Sunday," she said, repeating what she had said earlier. "Never in trouble with the law."

Verde tried to console her as her eyes welled up with tears.

She invited Verde to stay for dinner, but he felt awkward and told her he had to get back to the office for police business. As Verde was about to leave, she took hold of his hand. "I'm going to say a novena tonight at Saint Bartholomew Church for Ralphie and a prayer to Saint Anthony for you to help you find him. Please find him," she said, wiping the tears from her eyes. "He's all I have left."

"I'll do my best," he said solemnly as he left.

This was the part of the job Verde hated. He did not like to make promises he knew he couldn't keep. He had a strong inclination that her grandson had got mixed up in something ominous and that she would never see him alive again.

***

The sun was setting over the tall downtown buildings in the distance. On his way back to his office, Verde drove through his old neighborhood. As he passed by De Pasquale Avenue, he saw one of the boys from the neighborhood who he had arrested years earlier for selling counterfeit Rolex watches and Gucci handbags. It was Gino Lisi.

He pulled over. When his childhood friend recognized him, he came over to Verde, who rolled down the passenger side window. They went down memory lane, talking about who had died, who was in jail, who made it good and moved away, and who had been "whacked." They talked about the recent gangland murder of mobster Richard "Dickie" Callai and the Bonded Vault robbery. He said everyone on the Hill was tight-lipped about both crimes, but "theories up here about who pulled both crimes are a dime a dozen."

"What ever happened to Jennifer Del Marco?" Verde asked, with a broad smile.

Gino also smiled as he cupped his hands in front of his chest. "Mar-done, what a rack she had. I get a hard-on just from you mentioning her name. Jennifer married some guy in the construction business and lives in the suburbs. She's still very pretty, but she gained a lot of weight. Her ass is this wide," he said, extending his hands as far apart as they would go.

As Verde left, he told Gino to stay out of trouble. As he continued his drive through the old neighborhood, he became introspective.

Old feelings surfaced along with good and bad memories. It was funny, he thought, as he and Geno were reminiscing about the "good old days" how it had awakened a vision of Jennifer gliding down Atwells Avenue on a sunny summer afternoon. For him, the memory conjured up a vanishing era and many of the events of his past and the path that took him to this place and moment in time.

He was no longer that naïve young man. He now knew it was a labor in vain trying to recapture his past and those feelings and pangs of adolescence that were long gone, along with the innocence of his youth. Above all else, maybe Jennifer reminded him of a time when his future and destiny lay before him and all he had to do was reach out and take that brass ring. With his unbridled ambition and perseverance, he could shed and escape the lot in life that had trapped many of his childhood friends, including his brother. Growing up he held the steadfast believe that he could become the master of his own universe and shape his own destiny and station in life.

He arrived back at his office. As the memories of his past faded, he wondered what Jennifer really looked like now.

"So much for wet dreams," he thought.

Little did Verde know at the time that he would soon meet a woman as sexy and beautiful as the Jennifer he remembered who would satisfy all the wet dreams of his childhood libido.

Occam's Razor

The next morning, Verde drove to the Riverside section of East Providence. He passed by Crescent Amusement Park until he reached the end of Bullocks Point. He turned down a narrow road that was paved with white crushed clam shells to the address where all Imperatore's luxury and sports cars were registered.

The small, yellow clapboard house was fifty feet from Narragansett Bay. The garage, which appeared to have been a recent addition, was twice as large as the house. In front of the house were several state and local police vehicles and a light-gray state police Mobile Forensic Crime Lab cruiser. Red crime-scene tape had been strung along the telephone poles in front of the house.

State Police Detective Sergeant Richard Dunn looked up as Verde viewed the Imperatore file he had put together the day before.

Sergeant Dunn was a twenty-year veteran of the state police. He was short and overweight, with a receding hairline that displayed a horseshoe effect on his Marine-style haircut. "The feds are here," Dunn said to State Police Detective Lieutenant Rose Stone. "I wonder who it is."

Detective Stone was the detective in charge of the investigation. She looked up and recognized Verde. Immediately, her expression changed to one of disgust and contempt. She admired his investigative skills but detested his egotistical, headline-grabbing approach to law enforcement.

Detective Rose Stone was tall, lean, and athletically built. She jogged and worked out at a gym several days a week. Her short chestnut-brown was cut into a short trendy airstyle. Her foreboding eyes were dark and piercing. She had a master's degree in criminology and was attending law school at night. Her father was a retired special prosecutor for the Rhode Island Attorney General's office. Her mother was a former Miss Rhode Island and was now an aide for the speaker of the Rhode Island House of Representatives. Rose had inherited the best traits from both parents.

Although she was beautiful, she seldom wore more than basic makeup and dressed in a dark-green matronly business suit while on duty. She wanted to be accepted for her skills as a detective and hid her femininity for the sake of her career. She seldom smiled or discussed her private life, even with the other women on the force. Her aloofness and cold demeanor earned her the unflattering nickname many of the state police officers called her—the Ice Princess.

The men she dated were attracted to her for her beauty but were put off by her "always on the job" mentality. Her dates felt like suspects, and their conversations resembled interrogations. Now, in her early thirties, she seldom dated and had resigned herself to furthering her career and forsaken the pursuit of a husband and starting a family.

Verde got out of his vehicle. The fog was just lifting. A flock of seagulls were squawking as they flew overhead. The sounds of waves were crashing over the shoreline, and Verde took in a deep breath of the thick salty air.

"Jesus Christ!" Dunn said to the other officers. "What the fuck's he doing here?"

As Verde walked down the cobblestone path toward the officers, Detective Stone walked into the house, mumbling a barely audible obscenity that sounded like the word "asshole."

"What's up with that?" an East Providence police officer asked Sergeant Dunn.

"There's no love lost between those two. They have a history. She was the lead investigator on a big case when Verde was one of us. Colonel Stone, no relation to her, kicked it upstairs and put Verde in charge. The colonel has never been a big fan of women on the force. Even though she did most of the legwork on the investigation, when the case was solved, Verde received most of the credit and a promotion, and Stone got passed over.

"More like fucked over," one of the other state troopers interjected as Verde walked over to where the officers had gathered.

"What are you doing here, Hollywood?" Dunn asked in a condescending tone as the other officers smirked. "There's no TV cameras or newspaper reporters here."

"Just observing," he said, disregarding Dunn's snide remark.

"Good, and don't contaminate our crime scene. There's *real* investigative work being done here at this crime scene," he said.

"I wasn't aware, as of yet, that it had been determined that this was a crime scene," Verde said smugly. "Do you mind if I look around?"

"Knock yourself out," Dunn said.

Verde entered the garage, and as he passed by the highly polished red Mercedes convertible sports coupe, he ran his finger along the side. He observed the neatly stacked cans of oil and detailing accessories, all of which were assembled with their labels facing outward. All of his mechanic and gardening tools were neatly arranged on pegboards except for one, a pair of tree loppers. "Obsessive-compulsive neat freak," Verde thought. Then he noticed something that stirred his curiosity. All the cabinet drawers were partially open, as if someone had been rummaging, looking for something.

When he entered the small kitchen, he smelled the faint acrid, cloying smell of what appeared to be bleach. He knelt and leaned over and noticed an area in the middle of the floor that had appeared to have been recently cleaned. He swiped his rubber glove over the floor, smelled it, and then placed the tip of his finger to his tongue. He took one of the kitchen chairs that had been hastily put back and was not in alignment with the other chairs. Once again, he ran his finger over the seat cover, smelled it, and placed the tip of his finger to his tongue. Immediately, Verde had a hunch, a growing suspicion, and his premonitions were seldom wrong.

A member of the forensic team who had been observing Verde wondered why he kept nodding to himself as if he was acknowledging something. Verde went outside and opened a trash bin. Hidden under the regular trash were two empty plastic gallon jugs of Clorox bleach and black cable ties that were cut in half. Sloppy, unprofessional "cleaners" he thought to himself as he nodded once again. He then went back into the garage, picked up the tree loppers, and smelled them.

Sergeant Dunn entered the house and talked with the member of the forensic team who had been observing Verde.

Verde was walking into the backyard when Dunn stopped him. "Okay, Verde, what is it that you think you know?"

"I guess you were right, but even a broken clock is right twice a day."

"Right about what, smartass?"

"This is a crime scene."

"Okay, Hollywood, how'd you come to that conclusion?"

"Ask your forensic team to take the empty gallon jugs of bleach from the trash cans and the tree loppers in the garage. Check them with luminol for traces of blood, but not before dusting them for prints. Also test the middle of the kitchen floor and the chair to the left of the table with luminol."

"We were going to get around to that, Hollywood! Remember you're just an observer here. Don't come here and tell us how to do our job."

"Just trying to be helpful," Verde said, tongue in cheek. "After all, we're all *real* detectives," he said, mocking what Dunn had said earlier.

Detective Stone approached Dunn, and he told her what Verde had advised.

"Good morning, Agent Verde," Stone said in a cordial, businesslike manner. "What is it that you think you know?"

"Nothing concrete as of yet. I'm sure your team would have gotten to it...eventually."

"Sergeant Dunn, do whatever Agent Verde advised and bring me the results.

Verde walked in the direction of the small dock. A white speed boat was moored to it, bouncing in the waves. As he was about to walk on the dock, he noticed something odd about the topography of the land leading to the dock. He lifted up several pieces of sod and noticed that the loam underneath had recently been disturbed. He motioned for Stone and Dunn to come over.

"Do you have a metal detector in the lab truck?"

"Yes, we do," Stone said.

"Good. Have one of the forensic team sweep the backyard and mark all the areas that register an indication."

A short while later, one of the forensic team swept the backyard, placing markers each time the metal detector indicated that something metallic was buried underneath the soil. An East Providence officer began digging at the first site that was marked. About eighteen inches deep, he hit a metal object. Once he had cleared enough soil from around the object, he removed a heavy, dark-green metal pillbox with words and numbers printed in discolored yellow lettering, which stated "Property of the US Army," and some numbers.

All the officers came to the backyard to observe the development. The East Providence police officer donned a pair of rubber gloves and opened the pillbox.

"What was that, a lucky guess, Hollywood?" Dunn said, looking in the direction of Verde.

Verde didn't answer him. The officer began removing neatly wrapped plastic bags and placed them on the grass. In the bags were expensive watches, gold and silver jewelry, and various-sized colored gemstones. Then he removed a dozen plastic storage sheets, each containing nine one-ounce ingots of pure twenty-four-carat gold. The last item in the bottom of the box was so heavy the officer had to use two hands to remove it. It was a canvas bag marked US Mint. He opened it up by untying the drawstrings and removed a handful of shiny silver dollars.

Verde leaned over and smiled. "Are all the coins uncirculated Morgan silver dollars dated 1887?"

The officer looked up at Verde astonished. "Yes, how did you know?"

"*Just lucky*, I guess," Verde said, looking over at Sergeant Dunn, mocking him once again.

When the forensic team dug up the other pillboxes, they found similar valuables in each container. Verde went to examine the speedboat. Once again he smelled the faint odor of bleach. On his way back toward the house, he looked down at a row of thorny rose hip bushes. Then he noticed a small object under one of the bushes. He turned it over with his pen and smiled, but it was with mixed emotions because he knew what it meant.

With the assistance of Occam's Razor and deductive reasoning, it all became clear to Verde what had transpired. He knew he was correct, but it did not give him any solace. As a hardened law enforcement agent, he had witnessed the aftermath of numerous murders. He was almost desensitized to the brutal nature of his work. It was how a person in his profession emotionally survived and maintained composure and sanity. However, in this case it had taken on something personal. After all, he had promised Imperatore's grandmother that he would find her Ralphie.

He took out the photograph that Imperatore's grandmother had given him. As he studied the facial features, he went into a trance. He heard the horrific screams and envisioned Imperatore's assailants cutting off his fingers, one at a time, as they tortured him to find where the treasure was buried.

Dunn noticed that Verde was in a trance looking out over the water. As he approached him, Verde snapped out if it and began examining the area around the rose bushes. "Okay, Verde, what did you find now?"

"I don't know; you tell me," Verde said smugly.

"What the hell's that supposed to mean?"

Detective Stone walked over to them in a quickened pace as she saw Verde pointing something out to Dunn.

"If you look under the second rose bush," he said to Dunn, "I think that's Imperatore's thumb."

Stone immediately called over a member of the forensic team to bag and tag the evidence. When she looked up, Verde had vanished. She looked toward the front of the house and saw him talking on his car phone.

***

A half hour later, a chauffeured state police vehicle and a black Ford Bronco from the attorney general's office pulled up in front of the house. Colonel Walter Stone, head of the state police, and Attorney General Julius Michaelson stepped out of their vehicles.

The colonel was dressed in full state police regalia, and with his wide-brim state police Mounty-style hat, he stood nearly six foot six. His surname of Stone suited him well. His bold, chiseled features appeared to have been carved in stone, and to the best of anyone's recollection, no one had ever seen him even crack a smile.

The officers on the scene watched intently as Verde, Colonel Stone, and the attorney general were in deep discussion. The attorney general got into his car and left. The colonel motioned for Detective Stone to come over, with a nonchalant wave of his hand.

"Detective Stone," the colonel said in a monotone voice, "I know you're acquainted with Agent Verde."

"I am, sir."

"The attorney general and I concur with Verde's assessment that this crime scene has state and federal implications far greater than a missing person's case. This crime scene is now under joint federal and state jurisdiction. There is evidence that this crime scene is linked to the Bonded Vault robbery. I am assigning you to assist the bureau as our liaison with the feds until the investigation is concluded."

With those words, the colonel and his chauffeur left. Stone didn't appear to be happy with his directive. She placed her hands on her hips and backed away from Verde. "Since you seem to know what happened here, if we're going to work together, perhaps you can bring me up to speed. What went on here, and why does it have state and federal implications?"

"If we're going to work together, Rose, you can call me Jay."

Detective Stone was put off by his overly friendly demeanor, believing it to be too informal and unprofessional.

"If it's all the same, Agent Verde, I'd prefer it to keep our relationship strictly on a professional basis. You may call me Detective Stone."

Verde looked into Stone's dark-brown piercing eyes and shook his head. "Okay, *Detective Stone*. Then let's get right down to business. Do you know what Occam's Razor is?"

"I know of the theory, vaguely. How does that apply to what the colonel said?"

"Occam's Razor is a method of deductive reasoning which postulates that when you have more than one competing theory, what appears to be the obvious answer is usually the correct one. The problem as I see it with what happened here is that there are several plausible scenarios. Ralph Imperatore had the perfect cover to keep him under the radar of law enforcement. He worked as a substitute teacher in Providence. In reality, his hidden profession is that of a high-level fence."

"What happened to him?"

"He was tied up in the kitchen and his assailants began cutting off his fingers with the tree loppers in the garage until he told them where some of the valuables were buried. After he lost too much blood, he probably became unconscious before he could tell them the locations of all the buried treasure. After he was no longer of any use to them, they whacked him. They took him out in his own boat and dumped him in Narragansett Bay. The 'cleaners' were armatures. They tried to erase any traces of their deeds with bleach. In their haste to dispose of all the body parts, they dropped his thumb in those rose bushes."

"What evidence is there linking his murder to the Bonded Vault robbery?"

"The bright, uncirculated 1887 Morgan silver dollars. Dozens of them were found strewn on the Bonded Vault floor. The robbers must have dropped some of the contents of one of the bags on the floor and didn't have the time to pick them up."

"Who do you think killed Imperatore?"

"Well, that's one of many competing theories. The first scenario is that the men who robbed the Bonded Vault fenced part of the valuables with Imperatore. After they got the cash, they returned and stole back some of the valuables they had fenced. Maybe whoever killed him were holding out on some of their accomplices. In that case, the ones who got cut out may start an internal war among themselves.

The second scenario is that the mobsters who had their valuables robbed in Bonded Vault found out that Imperatore had fenced the loot. They figured they'd take back some of the valuables that were stolen from them. If that scenario is true, they probably tortured Imperatore not only to find the location of the buried treasure but also who had fenced the loot.

Right now, they're probably looking to torture and then whack the other participants in the robbery. You want to hear the scariest scenario?"

"I can hardly wait," Stone said, raising her eyebrows.

"Patriarca figured out that some of the Bonded Vault robbers were skimming some of the valuables before he got his cut. He sent out a crew to get back the valuables and whack Imperatore, but not before he told them who fenced the goods. If that scenario is the correct one, the Old Man will whack *all* the Bonded Vault robbers who betrayed him and in the process sever all links tying him to the heist. And then do you know what will happen, Rose?"

"No, enlighten me."

"There'll be a gangland war, and the bodies will pile up."

"What evidence is there to link Patriarca to the Bonded Vault robbery?"

"Occam's Razor. A heist of this magnitude could never have happened on the Old Man's turf without his blessing and receiving his piece of the score, his tribute. No one would pull a robbery like this without it being sanctioned by Patriarca unless they had a death wish."

"So, how do we proceed?"

"Linking Patriarca to the Bonded Vault robbery is the big prize. If we can catch the crew who killed Imperatore, and if they are the Bonded Vault robbers, we'll cut a plea deal with them to testify that Patriarca sanctioned the robbery and have him on conspiracy and possibly RICO charges. Believe me, they'll cut the deal rather than get an M-1 life sentence. But, Patriarca knows this, and we'll have to find them before he does."

"Is this all supposition? How'd you come up with all these possible theories?

"Occam's Razor. I'd like you to do me a favor. Have the forensic team get a blood sample from Imperatore's thumb and a blood sample from his grandmother—I'll give you her address—and see if it's a match. She told me that her grandson was all she had left in this world. Use some tact and break it to her gently. Our investigation will start tomorrow."

Once again, Rose thought, an investigation that had been assigned to her was reassigned by her superiors to Verde. Now she despised him even more.

When the Cat's Away...

Six months earlier

Remy Gerard was a loyal member of the Patriarca crime family. He was feared and respected by the criminal underworld and known by law enforcement and mobsters by his alias, The Frenchman. He was a well-liked, stand-up guy, and a man of his word who was not to be underestimated or trifled with. He would not think twice, have any remorse, or lose any sleep about putting two to the back of the head of anyone who crossed him or if the Old Man ordered him to whack someone. Although he was the Old Man's "right hand man" he could never become a "made guy." In order to become a made member of the Mafia's La Cosa Nostra, both of a candidate's parents had to be of Italian decent.

The Frenchman was in his forties, with a round, jovial face, rugged build, broad shoulders, and a receding hairline. He was not a typical "wise guy." He was intelligent, level headed, even tempered, and articulate. All his scores, ranging from high-end robberies to hijacking, were carried out with military precision.

He had been cultivating the Bonded Vault robbery for many years, only waiting for the proper time and the right situation. Very few knew, not even those in law enforcement, that the old red-brick building on Cranston Street in Providence was the secret location of 146 secret mob vaults containing millions of dollars of illegal undeclared valuables.

He felt that the time and conditions were right for him to pitch the heist to the Old Man. As a loyal member of the Patriarca crime family, the Frenchman knew he could not carry out this heist without the Old Man's blessing. Patriarca and his underboss had just been released from prison for conspiracy to commit murder after ordering the execution of a small-time bookie, Willie Mafeo. Mafeo had refused to pay his tribute for his gambling operation and disrespected one of Patriarca's, "cappos," Henry Tameleo, who tried to mediate the dispute.

Patriarca knew that since his release from prison, he was under constant surveillance. He only talked with those in his inner circle and conducted business through "buffers," fearing that he may be set up or recorded. After his release from prison, he vowed he would never be incarcerated again and took the necessary precautions to ensure that it would never happen.

The Frenchman asked for a sit-down with the Old Man through one of his trusted intermediaries. He went to meet with Fredrick Carusoe, known in the underworld as Freddie or Mister C. Mister C. operated the Old Man's *legitimate* business on Atwells Avenue in Providence called the Coin-O-Matic, a vending-machine operation.

City, state, and federal authorities knew that the Coin-O-Matic building clad in faux black marble was the New England headquarters of Patriarca's empire. Usually, the Old Man could be seen standing outside the building, always dressed casually, with an unfiltered cigarette dangling in a downward position from his lips. Since his release from prison, he was seldom seen outside. He always wore a pair of black penny loafers and his signature white athletic socks. To the outsider, they may have thought he always wore white socks because he was out of touch with fashion. In reality he wore white sox because he had diabetes.

A dusting of light snow had fallen the night before. As the Frenchman approached the entrance of the Coin-O-Matic, rock salt crushed under foot as he walked. Rows of pinball, video, and cigarette vending machines cluttered the small building. The Frenchman was told that Mister C. was in the back overseeing and counting boxes containing cartons of cigarettes from a large unmarked white truck with North Carolina plates. All the cigarettes had counterfeit Rhode Island tax stamps and would be distributed throughout New England in the Old Man's vending machines.

The Frenchman greeted Mister C. without saying a word. He just nodded his head, and Freddie did the same. Although the building was swept for bugs by a private security firm each week, they did not speak until they went for a walkabout down the back streets of Federal Hill. Mister C. relayed the request to the Old Man for the sit-down, and it was arranged for the following week.

*

A week later the Frenchman arrived at Freddie's mansion on Ocean Road in Narragansett, Rhode Island. The first floor of his Tudor-style home had a stone facade with white stucco on the second floor and a red California clay-tile roof. The grounds were manicured, and a tall fieldstone wall encompassed the property. Tall majestic stone columns bordered the entrance to his estate, with a crushed-stone driveway.

By the outward appearance, Mister C.'s mansion fit into the neighborhood of expensive homes near the ocean. However, his home was a fortress outfitted with unbreakable glass, hardened doors, and a state-of-the-art security and surveillance system. The phone lines were swept each week for bugs.

It was an unseasonably warm day for February in Rhode Island. The meeting had been set up in a sunroom in the rear of the mansion, overlooking a small koi pond and manicured conifers and ornamental shrubs. The Frenchman had arrived early, and one of Freddie's servants brought out a silver urn with hot coffee, cream, and Italian pastries. On a separate tray were the Old Man's favorite sugar-free diabetic cookies.

A late-model black Cadillac pulled into the estate and came to a stop at the front entrance. The Old Man's chauffeur, who doubled as his bodyguard, opened the car door. Mister C. greeted Patriarca at the entrance.

The Old Man was an unimpressive figure. He was five foot seven with a thin, frail frame. His black hair was interspersed with gray and slicked back. He was all gray at the temples. He wore a light-brown trench coat, brown hat, tan slacks, white shirt, and a beige cashmere sweater.

Patriarca lived his life abiding by the tradition of old-school Mafia principles, which postulated discretion, avoiding an ostentatious lifestyle of wearing designer clothing and owning expensive luxury motor vehicles, to keep a quiet, low profile, and above all else, to avoid the limelight.

One of Mister C.'s servants took Patriarca's hat and overcoat. He sat down across from the Frenchman, lit up a cigarette, and took in a deep drag. "Freddie told me what you had in mind," he said slowly. "Convince me why I should sanction this thing."

As the Frenchman began laying out his reasoning, his enthusiasm grew to the point that he was taking so fast that the Old Man motioned for him to slow down. He took a deep breath and continued. "Most of the guys who keep their valuables in the Vault have been light or skimming on your cut and many stopped turning anything in at all while you were away in prison."

"Like who?" Patriarca asked in a quiet voice, almost rhetorically.

"Bingo, from Cranston has been shy. Henry from Johnston stopped turning in anything at all. Most of the bookies have been light.

Dickie has been shaking down most of them. He figured that you'd die and prison and he'd take over. We would have whacked Callei a long time ago, but we didn't want to start a war with his crew when you were in prison."

"That was the right decision," the Old Man said, taking a nibble of a cookie and a sip of coffee. "I know that you and your crew have been loyal to me and good *earners* when I was away. You don't have to tell me what's been going on in my absence. My eyes and ears are everywhere. I know Callei was *shakin' down* everyone when I was away. Does that punk think he's me?" he asked, raising his voice slightly. What do you think, Freddie?"

Mister C. just nodded his head.

"I know you're a serious man, Gerard, and I like your plan. If I give the green light, it won't be for a while. *Friends of ours* have vaults there, and we wouldn't want to start a war. If we proceed, I'll give them time to clean out their vaults. I have a vault there with a Thompson submachine gun, not for protection, for nostalgia. It belonged to Al Capone. One of my goombahs got it from Capone's underboss, Frank Niti. If I give you the okay, I want all *stand-up guys* who'll do the time if they get caught and not rat. Capiche! I'm never going back to prison."

"I understand, Ray. I have a good crew in mind."

"You have any idea what's in the Vault?" Patriarca asked, with a cunning smile.

"I'm just guessing, maybe three mil."

The Old Man smiled and took another deep drag from his cigarette. "Try close to twenty million or more."

"Really. I guess you're the only one who really knows. What do you want me to put aside for you?"

"I don't want Bingo's duffel bags full of cash or the gold and silver coins, stamps, or jewelry. I want all the jewels in a certain locker and most of the twenty-pound blocks of gold bullion in another. I'll give you those lockers numbers that I want you to hit first. You see any obstacles…problems we'll have to take care of before you hit the Vault?"

"Only one, Dickie Callei, and maybe some guys in his crew. After we hit the vault, he'll be slapping guys around trying to figure out who pulled the heist to get a piece."

A cat-ate-the-canary smile appeared on the Old Man's face. "You let me worry about Callei. He's been living on borrowed time, and as far as his crew, if you cut the head off the shepherd, the sheep will scatter."

The Old Man stood up and shook the Frenchman's hand, signaling that the meeting was over. "Keep in touch with Freddie. He'll let you know when and if you can do this thing." And with those words, the Frenchman left.

After the Frenchman left, Freddie moved closer to the Old Man. "Ray, what do you think?"

"The reward is worth the risk."

"He's right about Dickie. He'll be a problem."

"When the cat's away…the mice turn into rats. Those vermin have been getting fat at my dinner table," Patriarca said, rubbing his chin as he thought. "There's been an ongoing beef between Dickie and Bobo. They hate each other. Have someone put a whisper in Bobo's ear…give him a little push. Let Bobo know that I want a brutal example made out of Dickie. We'll send a clear message that I'm back and who's in charge. After he's gone we'll see if anyone's light again, and they'll be scarred shitless to retaliate after the Vault is hit. Come on; let's get lunch. George's Restaurant on the water."

"Sounds good to me, Ray."

Gangland

Light snow had been falling the evening of March 14, and on that night, the mean streets would live up to their name.

The Acorn Tap was a local barroom, a late-night gathering place for the underworld. It was located in the bowels of Federal Hill. Wise guys, mob associates, and wannabes would roll in after the nightclubs, strip joints, and restaurants had closed. After a night out gambling or checking out of a hotel with their girlfriends or gumattas, the denizens of the Hill would go to the Acorn Tap to get an afterhours night cap or discuss business.

The Acorn Tap was operated by Frank "Bobo" Marrapese. He was a mob associate who operated illegal gambling, loan sharking, and the extortion rackets. He was known in the underworld as a man prone to uncontrollable rage and vicious acts of ultraviolence, especially when collecting a debt. Marrapese was a burly man weighing two hundred pounds and standing only five foot eight. He had a large overly round head, receding hairline, and wore thick black-framed glasses.

It was 2:30 a.m., and the mean streets were deserted. The Acorn Tap was almost empty except for Bobo and a few members of his crew. The small dimly lit bar smelled like stale beer mixed with the cloying odor of disinfectant and urinal cakes emanating from the open door to the men's room.

Marrapese placed the barstools and chairs up on the round wooden tables and swept the floor underneath. He looked up to the old yellowed clock above the bar. It was almost closing time. He knew that, like clockwork, Richard "Dickie" Callei would come strolling in just before closing time, and that predictable routine would prove to be his undoing.

Callei walked into the bar with a slow but deliberate gate in his stride, with an air of arrogance and superiority. He acknowledged the others in the bar by just nodding his head. Two of Marrapese's crew, Frank Martellucci and Bobby Ferle, were passing time playing gin. They looked up and just nodded their heads in Callei's direction.

Dickie had been to a pre–Saint Patrick's Day party, and he was dressed for the occasion. He wore a green checkered polyester sports jacket, dark green pants, white shirt, and tan buckskin loafers. He took off his jacket and placed it on a rack next to the men's room.
Callei was in his early forties, of medium build and height, with long light-brown hair pushed back, resembling a lion's mane, and a neatly trimmed goatee.

Bobo walked up to his crew, took a mopeen from out of his apron, leaned over, and pretended to clean the table, all the while keeping an eye on Dickie. "We all set?" he asked in a voice slightly above a whisper. Callei was standing at the bar primping his hair as he admired himself in the barroom mirror.

Ferle looked in Callei's direction and back to Bobo and just nodded his head.

"Be with you in a minute, Dickie," Bobo said, with a sardonic grin on his face, winking to his crew.

Bobo went behind the bar and made Dickie his usual drink, a tall glass half filled with Southern Comfort Whiskey. Then Bobo took a couple of bites of the Italian grinder he had made earlier. Callei took a bottle of Robitussin AC cough syrup out of his pocket and emptied the contents into the glass. He took a long gulp, smacking his lips. The concoction of alcohol and codeine helped him come down and relax from all the amphetamines he had been consuming all evening like M&M's. As Callei was finishing his drink, he didn't notice that Bobo had gone to the front door and slid across the dead bolt.

Bobo slowly walked up behind Dickie and pulled a .38-caliber pistol from underneath his apron. He pushed it into Callei's back and fired five shots that echoed throughout the barroom. *Bang! Bang! Bang! Bang! Bang!*

Immediately, the back of Callei's white shirt was covered with blood as he dropped to the floor. The room smelled of burned gun powder, and thick white smoke covered the small room. Everyone's ears were ringing from the gunshots. The floor surrounding Callei's body was pooling with blood and in the dimly lit room appeared as black as ink. Suddenly, Dickie began twitching and convulsing.

Bobo calmly walked back behind the bar, put down the pistol, and finished his grinder.

Ferle jumped up quickly and picked up a chair ironically inscribed with *Prata's Funeral Home*. "That cocksucker ain't dead yet," he shouted as he began smashing Callei with the chair.

"Ay-oh, Bobby, stop," Marrapese shouted, with his mouth full of food. "That's a reflex. Believe me; he's dead. I got enough mess to clean up. Pull the car in front," he said to Martellucci. "I'll wrap him up. We'll take him to the hole you guys dug behind the golf course."

■■

They pulled up behind Pine Valley Golf Course in Rehoboth, Massachusetts. The dark, secluded area was known to the locals as "Lover's Lane." Ferle and Martellucci had dug a shallow grave earlier in the evening. They dragged the blood-stained lifeless corpse of Callei and tumbled him into the hole. Bobo took out a kitchen knife and repeatedly stabbed Dickie in the face and abdomen and left the long kitchen knife sticking out from his chest. Ferle picked up a few boulders that had been removed when they dug the hole and smashed Callei in the head, all the while laughing.

"They wanted an example made of him. Here's to you, Dickie," Martellucci said, picking up a large boulder with both hands and then thrusting it into the side of Callei's head. It struck him with such force that his head split open and gray matter oozed out. Then Bobo threw Callei's sports jacket into the hole and they left.

After they returned to the Acorn Tap, Bobo cleaned up the aftermath of the execution while Martellucci drove Dickie's car to Fall River with Ferle driving behind him and left it behind a Portuguese restaurant.

***

As the dim early-morning sun rose, a jogger saw the tire tracks and footprints in the light snow that led to the gravesite and called the Rehoboth Police.

The murder of Callei was reported in the late edition of the Providence Journal newspaper, stating some of the graphic details that led to his death. The chief of police in Rehoboth was quoted as saying that the "vicious way Callei was killed and the fact that the body was not covered indicated to him that whoever killed Callei wanted the body to be found. Usually when a mobster with Callei's reputation is murdered, the body is never found. It appears that someone in the underworld wanted the body to be found, and Callei's brutal death was sending a message."

***

March 17, Saint Patrick's Day

The day after Callei's murder, the FBI stepped up surveillance on the Hill, concentrating their effort on the area surrounding the Coin-O-Matic. They were hoping that someone would slip up and indicate who had killed Callei or give information that would implicate the Old Man in ordering the hit.

The Old Man had arrived at the Coin-O-Matic early in the morning. At first the FBI surveillance team were baffled and more than curious when they saw a steady stream of wise guys and mob associates coming and going all morning carrying packages. One man in particular was carrying a large box carefully as if to protect the contents inside. Video surveillance confirmed that the man had picked up the package at Scialo's Bakery on Atwells Avenue. Maybe, they thought, that all this activity had something to do with the execution of Callei. They called Verde and relayed the activities at the Coin-O-Matic. Verde laughed and told them the ironic meaning behind the activity. The irony amused the agents as Verde told them that the "top wop," the head of New England's La Cosa Nostra, was born on Saint Patrick's Day, and the large box from Scialo's Bakery was probably a birthday cake.

The weeks following Callei's death, Federal Hill was rampant with rumors speculating who had whacked Callei. Everyone was convinced that the Old Man had ordered the hit. They all knew that the brutal way in which Dickie was executed and the way the body was left sent a chilling gangland message that was clearly understood. He had left this life in the same way he led his life, a violent man dying violently.

Bonded Vault

It is better to have robbed and got caught
than to never have robbed at all.

—Robert "The Duce" Dussault

The Old Man had given the Frenchman the green light. Frank "Cadillac" Saleme and Nicholas Bianco, who had vaults under assumed names, as well as other wise guys in New England, were given the word to clean out their vaults. They sent envoys in with suitcases under the guise that they were putting valuables into the vaults when all the while they were cleaning them out discreetly so as not to draw suspicion from the Vault's owner, Sam Lavine. Mister C. went into the Vault to retrieve the Old Man's Thompson machine gun.

The Frenchman began assembling the crew for what would become every criminal's dream, the score of a lifetime. The first man he wanted to recruit was Robert "The Duce" Dussault. They became friends while serving time together in Walpole Prison. He was a career criminal, having spent half his thirty-four years in reform school or prison. He had taken down some major scores and was known in the underworld as a top-notch, thinking man's criminal. The Frenchman knew that the Duce could coordinate a robbery of this magnitude and would put aside his ego and take direction from him. He knew that the Duce was cool headed and a "stand-up guy," a criminal who would rather do time than cut a deal with law enforcement. But most importantly, he knew Dussault was not a "cowboy," who believed it was never worth doing a life sentence for killing someone during a robbery. He would be the only one that the Frenchman would allow to carry a weapon during the heist.

The Frenchman asked Dussault to meet him at the S & S Bar, a small bistro located at the lower end of Federal Hill. The Duce was reluctant to come to Providence. He was leery of the ruthless Providence mobsters. He had read about the brutal execution of Dickie Callei, but he knew he'd be safe with the Frenchman, who was a well liked, feared, and respected member of the Patriarca crime family.

The S & S was a small establishment frequented by regular patrons, wise guys, mob associates, and wannabes. When the Duce arrived, Remy, as the locals called the Frenchman, was seated at a private table against the wall.

The Duce walked in with an air of confidence. He was of medium height and build and good looking but not overly handsome. He had a receding hairline and a neatly trimmed mustache. Upon occasion he was known to sport a full beard. He was dressed casually with dark brown slacks, a tan sports jacket, a beige cotton shirt, and a highly polished pair of Cordovan shoes. Everyone would always remark that the Duce bore a striking resemblance to the singer Bobby Darren.

The Frenchman had a hamburger and a plate of French fries in front of him. As the Duce sat down, he doused the fries with malt vinegar and catsup. The waiter brought over two beers for them.

"You want something to eat?"

"No, thanks. I ate before I came."

Remy laid out the score in a voice slightly above a whisper, leaning toward the Duce as he spoke. "Any questions?" the Frenchman asked.

"Many. When is it going down?"

"Very soon, three weeks, a month, maybe."

"What's the merchandise?"

"Hard to say. For sure gold, precious gems, and wads of cash."

"What the total take?"

The Frenchman smiled and looked in both directions. "Twenty mil, maybe more, maybe a little less."

A grin appeared on the Duce's face. Then his smile disappeared, and his look of joy turned to one of trepidation. "Who's the owners of the vaults we'll be hitting?"

"Low-level mobsters, bookies, fences, no made guys."

Now the Duce's face expressed a real concern. "If that's the case, the most important question is," he said, turning around to make sure no one was listening, "did the Old Man sanction the heist? I'm not in unless he gave it his blessing. You know better than anyone how the boys in Providence like whacking people, especially after they seen all the *Godfather* movies about a dozen times. I don't want to end up like Callei."

The Frenchman laughed. "You have my word. The Old Man gave me the green light on the robbery. I know what he wants from the score, and it's a *big* piece."

"Okay, I'm in. Who else is in on the score?"

"All reliable guys. Remember JoJo from Walpole? He's in."

"I like JoJo," he said, finishing his beer. He motioned for the waiter to come over and ordered an espresso coffee with a shot of Sambuca.

"Your good friend Chucky Floyd is in."

"He's a psychopath, but he's good in a pinch if there's any trouble, and he can be trusted, but he does have a few issues," the Duce said, raising his eyebrows.

The Frenchman knew exactly what Dussault was talking about. Chucky could make people around him nervous. He had an obsessive-compulsive disorder for extreme cleanliness. He had a fear of germs and was constantly washing his hands. He was also bipolar with a Jekyll-and-Hyde personality. One minute he would be calm and relaxed, and the next he would want to slit someone's throat.

Floyd was short with extremely curly hair, as if he had received a tight perm. However, the Duce wouldn't think twice about putting his life in Chucky's hands. He knew Floyd was loyal and would never let him down or the other men in the heist.

The next men recruited for the heist were Skippy Burns and Bobby "Big Mac" Macari. Their assignments would be to steal cars and vans and acquire all the tools necessary for the robbery.

Big Mac was tall and lanky and the youngest member of the crew. He always wore bell-bottom pants, platform shoes, and tie-dyed T-shirts. His long brown hair was cut in a mop-top fashion, resembling the style of Paul McCartney of the Beatles. The last time Duce had seen him, he said jokingly, "Hey, hippie, get a haircut."

"We're going to need some bull work," the Frenchman said. "How about bringing in Jake Tarzianian?"

Duce took a sip from his espresso and gave Remy an odd look. "You mean Jake the Snake? He's one scary-lookin' motherfucker, and he's as sick as he looks."

"I know, but he's strong as a bull, and we'll need his strength to bust open the one-inch-thick steel vault doors."

"That's fine. Just don't put a gun in his hands. If something goes wrong, he's liable to accidently shoot us along with everybody else."

They both laughed. "That's why you're the only one who's going to be carrying a piece.
I figure we need two more men. I want to use one of the men in my crew, Jerry Fassbender."

Jerry Fassbender had a long criminal record. He was tall and well built and most of the time sported a reddish-brown neatly trimmed beard.

The Duce knew that Fassbender was a bona-fide tough guy. Even though he'd rather be playing softball for the city of Providence's softball team rather than pulling down scores, he was reliable, and he shook his head with a yes.

"The last guy I'd like to put on our crew is Mitch Lanoue."

"You mean Lucky Lanoue?"

Mitch "Lucky" Lanoue would be the oldest man recruited for the robbery, but certainly not the brightest. He was short in stature but possessed great strength, all brawn and no brain. The Duce had nicknamed him Lucky and the name stuck after they collaborated on one of their less-than-memorable robberies. Everyone now called him Lucky in the same way an obese man is called Slim and a giant of a man is called Tiny.

The heist during which Lucky received his nickname was to be a smash-and-grab with only a window of five minutes before the police would arrive. The high-end jewelry store was built like Fort Knox and could only be robbed while it was open, and the alarms were impossible to shut off. While the Duce and JoJo tied up the employees, it was Lucky's job to smash the display cases and grab as many valuable items as the short time allowed before the law arrived. They got away clean, but when it came time to divvy up the loot, Lanoue had grabbed coins and books of stamps instead of the most valuable items. Instead of the three men splitting about a hundred thousand, they had to settle for three grand each.

"I guess he'll be okay," Duce said. "As long as he doesn't have to think."

***

JoJo and Skippy stole all the vehicles for the robbery from New London, Connecticut. The Frenchman gave Skippy and JoJo $500 to purchase all the tools necessary for the heist. He didn't want them stealing the tools and getting pinched beforehand. Skippy had worked in the construction trade and had a working knowledge of all the tools necessary to break open the hardened-steel vault doors. They purchased industrial drills, sledge hammers, pinch and wrecking bars, and large reinforced wedges.

Every aspect of the robbery and each man's role was rehearsed many times. They all cased Bonded Vault and recorded each employee's times of entering and leaving. They planned and timed their separate escape routes. All the men were waiting for was the Frenchman to give them the word.

August 14, 7:00 a.m.

It was a typical hot and humid August day in Rhode Island. As Lucky, Big Mac, and JoJo loaded the tools into the van, Duce reminded Lucky of one final but important instruction.

"Remember what I told you, Lucky. We all call each other Harry. Don't use anyone's real name. Don't fuck up this score!"

"Sure, sure, sure," Lucky said, getting into the van.

They all set out to arrive at the Vault using different routes. Duce and Fassbender got into Skippy's Chevrolet Monte Carlo and sped off.

The Bonded Vault was located inside the Hudson Furs Storage Facility in a rundown section of Hoyle Square on Cranston Street in Providence. Across the street from the Vault was Central High School and a track and football field. The large dilapidated red-brick building was also the location of Louttit and What Cheer Laundry.

The Duce was dressed like a businessman with a light-gray checkered jacket, open collar white shirt, and black pants. He was clean shaven, sporting a neatly trimmed mustache, and teardrop sunglasses. He tucked a .38-caliber snub-nose revolver in his waistband and picked up a dark-brown valise. He pressed the buzzer next to the glass door entrance and the door opened.

When Dussault entered Sam Lavine's office, he was sitting behind his large oak desk. He looked up briefly, seemingly preoccupied with his paperwork. Lavine was a small man in his sixties, with receding brown but mostly gray hair. His secretary was sitting behind him, facing the wall processing and filing cleaning slips.

"I'm going into the Vault," Duce said nonchalantly.

Lavine opened the top desk drawer and removed a ledger with the number and names of the vault holders. "What vault are you going into?" he asked, without looking up.

Duce smiled. "All of them," he said, reaching into his waistband as he pulled out his pistol.

Sam looked up with a puzzled look on his face. Suddenly he became frozen with terror, and he sat up rigid in his chair as he stared down the barrel of Dussault's gun.

"You there," Duce said to Sam's secretary, "stand up and turn around. What's your name?"

"Ba-Barbara Ol-Olivia," she said, stammering. "Are those real bullets in that gun?"

"Listen carefully, Barbara," the Duce said, waving the gun in her direction. "You go and round up all the employees and bring them in here, and I mean everyone! If I hear any alarms or any funny business, Sam will be the first to see if the bullets in my gun are real, and you'll be the second, capiche!"

A very short while later, Barbara escorted Sam's sister-in-law and his brothers Hyman and Abraham into the office. The Duce removed several pillowcases from his valise and made everyone except for Sam put them over their heads. "Sam," Duce said, pointing the gun in his direction, "Buzz my friend Harry in."

Sam buzzed in Chucky Floyd, who had just put on a Frankenstein Halloween mask. The Duce stuck his head out into the corridor and motioned for Chucky to have everyone come in. "Now everyone shut the fuck up. This will be over in a short while and no one will get hurt! It ain't your money, so you got nothin' to lose…except your lives if you're stupid!"

Chucky held the door open as the parade of men came in quickly, carrying duffel bags that served a dual purpose: to carry in the tools and to carry out the valuables. JoJo remained in the van as a lookout.

Behind the large one-foot-thick vault door were 146 vaults. Most of the vaults were two-foot square with some smaller and some much larger. The men quickly found out that the most efficient way to break open the doors was with wrecking bars and sledgehammers. The Frenchman's intuition about bringing in Jake the Snake and Lucky paid off. They had discovered a method of smashing off the doors so quickly, they were having a contest to see who could break open a vault door faster.

The Duce stayed in Sam's office guarding the hostages. He could hear the sound of metal against metal and the banging of sledgehammers coming from the vault. Each time one of the heavy steel vault doors hit the cement floor, it gave off a distinctive ringing toll like a manhole cover hitting a hard surface.

In the meantime, the Duce was daydreaming about how he was going to enjoy his share of the heist. He looked over to Sam and remembered a piece of information the Frenchman had told him. "While we have time, Sam, you can give me whatever is in the strong box you keep in your desk."

Sam raised up his shoulders and offered a thin look of bewilderment, which the Duce saw right through. "I don't know what you're talking about."

"Don't be fuckin' cute, Sam. I know you keep petty cash in your office. Hand it over!"

Sam reluctantly removed a small metal box, placed it on the top of his desk, and removed a small roll of bills wrapped with an elastic band. "There's only a couple of hundred here…coffee money. You want that too?" he asked defiantly.

Duce laughed. "Of course. I want every last fuckin' dime in this joint! You holding out on me?"

"I swear to God," he said, raising up his right shaking hand. "That's all there is."

"Relax, Sam. I believe you," Duce said, placing the small roll of bills in his jacket pocket.

***

At first, Big Mac thought the contents of the locker he was about to clean out was worthless. Inside were six small metal Band-Aid tins with elastic bands tightly bound around them. This was one vault the Old Man told the Frenchman he wanted him to hit first, and he wanted all of the contents in that vault. He opened one box and poured the contents into his hand. He stood motionless and tapped Chucky on his shoulder to take a look. In his outstretched hand were diamonds, rubies, emeralds, pearls, and other assorted gems.

Chucky smiled and turned around quickly as Fassbender opened an oversized vault and checked the contents. "Harry, you gotta see this!"

The vault was loaded with shoe boxes. In the bottom of the vault was a large green duffel bag. This was another one of the vaults that the Frenchman had given the locker number to the men to open first. It belonged to a mob associate known as Bingo. He operated legal and illegal gambling operations and rigged charity events with mob shills at churches' feasts and bazaars. Each shoe box contained neatly wrapped fifty- and one-hundred-dollar bills. Each stack had a paper slip wrapped around it with scribbled figures like five, ten, and twenty thousand. Chucky looked on intently as Fassbender unzipped the duffel bag. Inside were smaller bills, wrapped five-, ten-, and twenty-dollar bills. He zipped up the bag and heaved it near the vault entrance and then emptied the shoe boxes of cash into one of their duffel bags.

For the men in the vault, it was surreal—the kind of score they could only have dreamed about or seen in movies—and now it was happening for them. The expressions on their faces, these hardened criminals, were like little children opening up one present after another on Christmas morning. Soon the vault floor was strewn with loose jewelry, gold and silver coins, cash, and gems.

Chucky went into the office and tapped Dussault on his shoulder. He was walking as if in a trance, with glazed-over eyes. He didn't even blink. An expression of wonder and joy was frozen on his face. "Harry," he said, coming back to the moment, "I'll watch them. Go in the vault and take a look."

When the Duce entered the vault, Jake was on his knees scooping up cash and other valuables, fumbling as he tried to put as much into the duffel bags as quickly as possible. Most of the vault doors had been opened except for two, and since the doors were against the vault wall, the men couldn't get enough leverage to pry them open. Jake was now sweating profusely as he kept smashing a sledgehammer into a large wedge to open the largest six-by-three-foot vault door. The Duce smiled and nodded his head. He knew this was the score of a lifetime. In his thoughts he was spending his share in resorts and on women, and visions of Vegas danced in his head. Then he went back to the office and told Chucky to tell the men to scoop up everything and make it snappy.

The best was yet to come. When Chucky returned into the vault, Jake had just opened the largest locker. "Look at this!" he shouted. "It's the mother lode!"

All the men came over quickly. Stacked neatly inside the vault were countless five-, ten-, and twenty-pound gold and silver bricks and over a dozen canvas bags marked "US Mint." Each bag was so heavy that Jake had to use two hands to pick each one up. When Lucky picked one up, the bottom tore out, sending mint Morgan silver dollars rolling over the vault floor.

After the men filled most of the duffel bags, Chucky looked at his watch. "All right, we got enough. Scoop up as much as you can. We're leaving in two minutes." The men began dragging the duffel bags down the corridor and loaded them into the vehicles. It took nearly ten minutes to load the gold and silver bricks and the canvas bags of silver dollars into their vehicles. They didn't bring enough duffel bags for all the valuables and left the vault floor strewn with loose cash and coins, small gold and silver ingots, gold and silver jewelry, watches, and other odd valuables. After the men left in their vehicles, Dussault waited inside for them to make a clean get away. Just before he left, he asked Sam for his driver's license.

"Listen up, everyone. I got Sam's ID. If any of you wants to be a hero and identify me for the cops, I know where Sam lives, and I know where you work. Even if I'm in the can, someone will pay you a visit, and you can use your imagination as to what will happen to you…and your children! Capiche?"

Everyone who was still wearing pillowcases over his or her head nodded.

"I'm going to lock all of you in the bathroom. You won't know when I'm leaving. Don't try to bust out for, let's say, twenty minutes.

The Duce had everyone hold onto each other and form a human chain leading them into the bathroom. Then he wedged a metal folding chair against the door. Just before he was about to leave, he tapped his gun against the door. "Remember what I said. Twenty minutes."

When the Duce left Bonded Vault, he jumped behind the wheel of Skippy's 1973 Monte Carlo and sped off. Skippy and Lucky were in the backseat and Fassbender was in the front passenger side. Each vehicle was given different escape routes. The Frenchman thought that it might draw suspicion if a parade of vehicles were all heading to Chucky's East Providence home at the same time.

When Dussault left, he headed down Cranston Street by Wiggins Village Housing projects. As he turned down Bridgham Street, he noticed that something was wrong with the steering. The Monte Carlo was handling irrationality, as if it had a mind of its own. The rear bumper of the vehicle was scraping the pavement, and the front tires were coming off the ground, making it impossible to steer the vehicle.

"What the fuck's goin' on?" Duce yelled to Skippy.

Burns smiled. "Must be all the gold and silver bricks and silver dollars in the trunk."

He pulled the vehicle over as best he could. He looked over and saw a half dozen black men leaning against a brick wall, who became more than interested in their presence. "Lucky, go in the trunk and redistribute the bags of silver dollars into the front and rear seats.

Lucky began grabbing the canvas bags of silver dollars out of the truck and placed them in the floor of the front and back seats. As he attempted to grab another bag, he tripped and the bag broke open, spilling dozens of coins onto the sidewalk and into the street. Skippy jumped out of the car and began helping Lucky pick up the coins.

Dussault looked at the silver dollars in the street and then at the black men who began walking in their direction. "*Jesus* Christ!" he said, rubbing his hands over his face. "Lucky jinxed us. We got the score of a lifetime, and we're gonna get pinched before we ever divvy up the loot!" He took out his gun and placed it on his lap. "If those Moulinyans think they're going to jack us, I'll put a bullet in every one of their fuckin' heads!"

Fassbender looked at the approaching men. Their leader seemed to be prodding them to follow him. "I know that coon," Fassbender said. "That's Tyrone Watkins. We served time in the can several years ago. Duce, you got any cash on you?"

"No. I mean yes," he said, remembering the small roll of bills he stuffed into his pocket from Sam's office.

"Give it to me. I'll take care of this."

Fassbender got out of the car. The black men began moving toward them quickly. Suddenly, Tyrone recognized Fassbender. He knew Jerry was connected to the mob, and he motioned for his posse to stop.

Tyrone came walking over to Fassbender and extended his hand. "Hey, Jerry, what's going down?"

"Nothing that you or your boys would even think about gettin' involved in," he said, looking back at the men in the street. They had almost picked up all the coins. He reached into his pocket and removed the small roll of bills. Then he shook Tyron's hand, transferring the money to him discretely.

Tyrone looked at the roll of money in his hand. "What's this for, Jerry?"

"For you and your crew to forget what you just saw. We were never here. Got that?"

"You know the way I roll, Jerry. We'd never help the *man*."

"Come on, Jerry," Duce said. "Let's go!"

"Later, Jerry," Tyrone said, smiling.

"Later, Tyrone," Fassbender said, jumping into the car.

As Dussault sped off, he kept checking the rearview mirror to see that they were not being tailed. Once he was on the highway, he breathed a sigh of relief. As he headed toward Chucky's house, he confided with the others. "No need to spoil the moment and tell the others about this incident."

The all agreed to keep the incident among themselves.

The Score of a Lifetime

The Frenchman's Lincoln Continental Mark Four was parked in front of Chucky's Golf Avenue ranch house in East Providence when Duce and his crew arrived. The others who arrived before had already unloaded most of the valuables from the heist. Dussault backed into the driveway as Fassbender, Lucky, and Skippy unloaded the gold and silver bricks and the bags of Morgan silver dollars.

The inside of the small house was stifling hot, but it didn't seem to bother the men, except for Lucky, who was constantly complaining as the sweat dripped off his forehead. The valuables were taken to Chucky's bedroom. The gold and silver bricks, along with the canvas bags of silver dollars, were placed on the floor, and the jewelry, gems, and cash were dumped on his bed.

There were many varied-size small boxes that were unopened. Jake ripped open the boxes rapidly and dumped the contents on the bed. Many of them contained gold and silver jewelry, collector coins in Plexiglas display holders, and high-end watches. Then Jake came upon an old cigar box that was wrapped with silver-colored duct tape. He unraveled the duck tape and examined its contents before he dumped the contents on the bed. The men all looked at each other in silence as he poured a cascade of medium to large-size diamonds, rubies, emeralds, and other precious gemstones on the bed.

"Wow," Dussault said to the Frenchman. "There must be a half a mil, maybe more in street value, just in that box!"

The men formed an assembly line to count the cash. Big Mac sat on a reclining lounge chair with a calculator, notebook, and pencil to record the figures. Jake, JoJo, and Fassbender separated the large bills from the small ones, counted the totals, and called them out to Big Mac. When it came time to count the neatly wrapped stacks of cash Fassbender had taken from the shoeboxes, they realized that the totals on the slips of paper on the outside were accurate, and they just read the numbers off to Big Mac.

The Frenchman sat in the corner of the room, sipping a beer. He looked over at the Duce, smiled, and gave him a thumbs-up. "Was I right, or was I right?"

"I gotta say," the Duce said, with a grin, "I thought you were bullshittin' when you said what the take would be. Now I think it might be even more than you thought. This is the score of a lifetime."

"Just remember, I have to give the Old Man his cut. He wants some of the gold bricks and all the precious gems that were in the metal Band-Aid boxes, but all the rest is ours to split up."

Big Mac totaled the figures twice. Each man would receive about six hundred thousand in cash. They didn't have enough bags for each man to carry out his cash, so Skippy went to a local supermarket to get paper shopping bags. The men agreed that they would wait for their share of the remaining valuables to be fenced to receive their share. The Frenchman had the men place the Old Man's cut in the trunk of his car. Then he had them load up all the other valuables into a van that would be hidden at a secret location known only to him and Chucky.

After all the men left, Dussault, Chucky, and his girlfriend decided that they would go to New York on a shopping spree before they went to Las Vegas.

On their drive to New York, Chucky wondered why Dussault did not bring along his girlfriend. "I thought for sure you'd bring her," he said, looking straight ahead at the road as he drove, "if only to keep my girlfriend company.

"We got an on-again, off-again relationship. The women in Vegas are beautiful…and willing. With the kind of money I'll be throwin' around, I'm goin' to get a real nice piece of ass. Besides, when you go to the beach, you don't bring along a bucket of sand, do you?" he said, raising his eyebrows.

Chucky laughed. "I see your point," he said, smiling.

■ ■

When they arrived in New York, they checked into an expensive hotel. That evening they ate at Mama Leone's Restaurant, an Italian restaurant off Fifth Avenue. Then they partied at several downtown nightclubs

The next morning, they went to a men and women's beauty salon. Chucky and Dussault had facials, manicures, and stylish haircuts. Chucky's girlfriend had her hair dyed and styled.

Later in the day, they went to a Fifth Avenue men's and women's haberdashery, where Duce and Chucky bought several three-piece custom suits and accessories. Chucky's girlfriend bought several dresses and pantsuits.

That evening they ate at Sullivan's Steak House, a restaurant frequented by mobsters. All evening, the Duce felt like a fifth wheel on a car, without a female companion. That would all soon change, he thought. With his new attire and plenty of cash, he would "hook up" as soon as he arrived in Las Vegas.

Mean Streets

It was the best of times on the mean streets of Federal Hill for the crew who participated in the Bonded Vault robbery. In the months that followed the brutal execution of mobster Richard "Dickie" Callei, it was also the worst of times for bookies and mob associates who had been light or delinquent on the Old Man's tribute while he was away in prison. They wondered who among them would be next. Needless to say, none of them were light after the brutal lesson was understood.

It was a time of mob justice exemplified by extremely cruel beatings and executions. Several members of Callei's crew who were "mouthing off" about their leader's demise were whacked and simply disappeared, mob style.

It was also a time of extortion of local business establishments on the Hill. Most of shakedowns of local businesses were carried out under the guise of being "asked" to join a national organization orchestrated by New York mobster Joseph Colombo. It was called the Italian American Civil Rights League. It was touted as an antidiscrimination and defamation organization for to "protect" Italians' rights. All establishments on the Hill were "strongly" encouraged to join at a hefty annual fee and display their membership posters in their storefront windows.

It was most importantly a time where all mobsters' loyalty came into question: a time of consolidation of power, reorganization, and reevaluation of all members of the Patriarca Crime Family from cappos down to street soldiers.

Above all else, it became a time of extreme paranoia. Suspicion of everyone and everything ran rampant on the mean streets. It manifested itself in that most mobsters never left home without carrying a gun, or two.

*

The Providence and state police had questioned most of the usual suspects who were capable of executing the Bonded Vault robbery and had not come up with any solid leads. In the late morning, Verde and Detective Stone were going to meet up with Providence detectives known by their street names Mark and Tom. Mark and Tom were the legendary Pac-Men of Providence, known for their relentless pursuit of criminals. Criminals regarded them as gangsters with a badge who wouldn't think twice about bending a law or two to catch them. They were regarded as sort of a deterrent to their own kind. Although they could coerce or beat a confession out of even the most hardened criminal, they were considered "honest cops" or as honest a cop could be on the mean streets. They never "shook down" criminals or accepted bribes to overlook their criminal activities.

Mark and Tom were in their early forties, stood over six feet tall, and had overly muscular physiques from their many hours of working out at the Downtown Providence YMCA. When Verde arrived, both were wearing their undercover attire. Mark was wearing a Vietnam-era army jacket, faded blue jeans, and light-tan construction boots. Tom was wearing a dark-blue nylon parker, bell-bottom dungarees, white Converse high-cut sneakers, and a Red Sox baseball cap. They both spoke with guttural

Providence accents and vernacular with the demeanor of street thugs, which made them blend in with the degenerates they hunted on the mean streets.

Mark and Tom got into the backseat of Verde's black Crown Victoria. He wore a dark blue suit, white shirt, and dark teardrop sunglasses. Detective Stone wore her usual mundane dark-green business suit. Her small-caliber weapon was in a holster on a wide black belt under her short jacket. Verde introduced Stone to the men, but they already knew who she was.

"Where are we off to first?" Verde asked, turning around.

"Peppermint Lounge, upper Broadway," Mark said, with a sadistic grin. "The Frenchman and some of his crew hang out there. We're gonna bust some balls."

At times, Tom was like an echo of his partner and would repeat certain phases that humored him. "Yeah, bust some balls," Tom said.

As they arrived, Mark and Tom got out first. "Aren't you comin' in?" Mark asked Verde.

"In a few minutes. You soften them up, and then we'll go in and bust some *balls*," he said.

After the detectives entered the lounge, Stone turned to Verde. "What are we waiting for?"

"Give Mark and Tom a few minutes to, how should I say, use their special brand of interrogation. Their uncouth methods may be crude, but they're effective. Then we'll come in and rent some space in their heads."

"Like the bad-cop, good-cop routine."

"Well, not exactly. You'll see."

It was almost lunchtime. The barroom was frequented by many Providence city workers, who spent an hour or two at lunch playing cards and dining on Italian grinders, pasta, and beer on tap. When Verde and Stone entered the lounge, the bartender recognized him and immediately turned around and kept his eye on his movements in the barroom mirror, which did not escape Verde's notice.

When they entered a small dining area off the main bar area, Tom was engaged in a "lively" conversation with Jerry Fassbender, the Frenchman, and two men whom Verde didn't recognize. The detectives had pulled up chairs behind the men who were playing Hi-Lo-Jack. On the table were several half-eaten veal and chicken parmesan grinders, bottles of Narragansett beer, and small bags of beer nuts.

The Frenchman was wearing a pair of black slacks and a light-green V-neck sweater. Fassbender, who worked for the Department of Public Works for the City of Providence was wearing khaki work clothes.

"Listen, fuckface," Tom said to Jerry, "I axed you a question."

Fassbender looked up with a false nervous smile. "Hey, Verde, can you put a muzzle on this rabid dog?" The other men at the table snickered.

"Sorry, can't help you, Jerry," he responded, raising his eyebrows. "Out of my jurisdiction."

Verde knew that both Fassbender and the Frenchman were members of the Patriarca Crime Family and more than capable of being involved in the Bonded Vault robbery, but nothing as of yet linked them to the crime.

"Good afternoon, gentlemen," Verde said, removing his sunglasses.

The Frenchman looked up briefly. The dealer let him in for a three bid, and he led off with the queen of diamonds. "Slow day, Verde?" the Frenchman said, without looking up from his cards.

"I was wondering what you're still doing in Rhode Island. If it was me, and I just robbed millions of dollars in cash, gold, and diamonds, I'd be getting a tan in the Bahamas or Vegas or maybe hiding so I don't get wacked like Imperatore or Callei."

Verde studied Remy carefully for any sign of recognition when he mentioned Imperatore's name, but the Frenchman's face was without expression.

The Frenchman scooped up the trick. "Here's the only diamonds I have," Remy said as he followed with the king of diamonds. "And I'm not hiding from anyone. It's not my style."

"Maybe," Stone said, "you're hiding in plain sight…keeping a low profile."

Mark picked up a package of beer nuts in front of Fassbender, poured a generous amount in his hand, popped them in his mouth, and then threw the bag of peanuts back on the table. Jerry took the package and placed it at the far end of the table, out of Mark's reach.

Remy took the trick and followed with the ace of diamonds. The other players threw in their cards, and he made his three bid.

"Playing Onleyville Hi-Lo-Jack, Remy?" Verde said. "First you play the queen, then the king, and then the ace. Little backward, but effective."

"Some might say just like you, backward but effective," the Frenchman said as the other men playing cards laughed.

"Keep mouthin' off, asshole," Mark said. "Very soon you'll be laughin' out the other side of your friggin' face!"

"Yeah, the other side of your friggin' face!" Tom repeated. "As I figure it, one or more of your crew will get nigger rich, and then I'll squeeze them by the balls, and believe me; they'll rat you out. Sooner or later all you goombahs fuck up, and when you do I'll be there. You can bet your ass on that!"

It was Fassbender's turn to deal. He dealt out the cards quickly and then looked at his hand.

"Good luck," the Frenchman said. "I'll be right here waiting for you."

"Always nice talking with one of the boys from the old neighborhood," Verde said to Remy as he made ready to leave.

The Frenchman would not let Verde leave without a little quid pro quo. "Hey, Verde, you been up to Danbury Prison to see your brother? What's he got left, two years on his bid?" he said with a snicker.

Verde would not leave without giving the Frenchman a quip of his own. "Next time I see you, maybe you'll be in the cell next to him. Then you can say hello to my brother for me. And you'll be in for a lot more than a two-year bid. Have a nice day, gents."

As they left, Mark pointed to his eye and then toward Remy and Jerry, and they understood the silent message.

***

After they left, the Frenchman looked at Fassbender and gave him the eye. He didn't know if Verde was just on a fishing expedition or if he had uncovered something concrete and was sending them a message that their time would soon be up.

***

They drove by the Old Man's headquarters, the Coin-O-Matic, and the Acorn Tap, a known mobster's hangout, as Mark and Tom gave a running commentary on the mobsters who frequented each establishment. They pulled up in front of the Federal Grill, a small breakfast and lunch restaurant. Mark went inside to see if anyone of interest was there. There were a few low-level street soldiers standing outside. When they recognized Verde, several of the men turned around. One of the men stared down Verde defiantly and then threw him the middle finger.

"Hey, Verde, one of your fan club," Tom said, smiling, which caused Detective Stone to grin and then quickly suppress her half smile.

No one of interest was inside, so they drove by De Pasquale Avenue and parked in front of Abies Bar. Mobsters and old Italians played cards and shot dice on the second floor of the bar. There was no one of interest inside the bar either, so they drove on. As they passed by the alleyway next to Abies Bar, a painful memory from Verde's past surfaced.

When Verde was fifteen years old, some punks confronted him in that alley. They gave him a vicious beating, and he received twenty stitches to close the wound to his head. When his brother came home, young Verde was looking for sympathy from his older sibling. Instead, his brother chastised him for not "standing his ground." He remembered his brother telling him that "if you don't fight back, the beatings would continue." He couldn't intercede on his brother's behalf "because those punks have older brothers, and the Old Man would get pissed if this small beef escalated into a war." A few weeks later, young Verde got word that the punks were looking for him again. On his way out each morning, he took a length of gas pipe from his basement, and when the punks confronted him again, he beat them senseless. That was the law of the land on the mean streets of

Atwells Avenue. And so the Verde boys earned a reputation that they were not men to be "fucked with."

He remembered what his father said to him after the altercation. When Verde's father found out what had happened, he understood, without condoning or condemning, what his son had done. His mother wanted to move away from the bad element before "both of our sons end up as gangsters or dead."

Verde's father said that they couldn't afford to move, and besides, "you can take the boy out of the Hill, but you can't take the Hill out of the boy!"

***

"Where do you want to go next, Verde?"

Verde's memory vanished as he came back to the moment. "Decatur Square."

"Who you lookin' for in the Square?" Tom asked.

"Freddie the Kook."

Detective Stone laughed. "Colorful name," she said, shaking her head.

"That's nothing," Tom said. "Up here we got Buckles, BoBo, Baby Shanks, Black Jack, Twitch, Mousie, and of course, the Moron, and I could go on and on."

Detective Stone turned around. "Why do they give a man a nickname like the Moron?"

"For the same reason they call the White House the White House," Tom said. In Marabella's case, he's called the Moron because he's an imbecile capable of outrageous irrational behavior.

"Verde, what do you hope to learn from Freddie?" Mark asked. "He's just a low-level fence."

"Maybe, if he can be played right, he may just be stupid enough to inadvertently give up a significant piece of intel."

They parked two blocks away from Decatur Bar. Next to the bar was a three-story tenement house. Freddie the Kook sold his "hot" merchandise from out of the basement and first and second floors of the building. A long alleyway led to the rear of the building. Several men in their late twenties guarded the entranceway to the alley. They were the Kook's enforcers, making sure no one robbed the place or skipped out without paying. Business was brisk that afternoon. Verde and the others observed patrons coming and going with suits, women's dresses, and small appliances ranging from toasters to color television sets.

"See that punk wearing the black sleeveless T-shirt?" Tom said. "That's the Kook's nephew, Rocco Assenzi. He's one psychotic, violent prick, pardon my language, Stone. He's extremely dangerous because he's a wannabe with something to prove, always trying to draw the attention of the wise guys who one day may need a sicko in their crew with his violent tendencies. One day they'll use him for extortion and collections."

Verde was familiar with Rocco's long rap sheet. He knew in time he would move up the mob chain. As long as Rocco's behavior did not draw any unnecessary attention or heat, his activities would not only be tolerated but encouraged, and one day rewarded.

"Rocco will be very uncooperative," Mark said. "We haven't got a warrant, and the Kook probably gave him instructions not to let anyone in who isn't there to buy hot stuff, and especially no cops."

"Maybe we should all go out and pay Rocco and his crew a visit," Verde said. "Strength in numbers."

"I'll take care of it," Stone said. "Did you think I was just along for the ride?"

Mark looked at Tom and smiled. "You got some balls on you, I'll give you that much. In all due respect, Rocco doesn't fear anyone or anything, especially someone with a badge. A year ago, some idiot downtown sent a rookie at night on foot patrol in the Square. Although we could never prove it, it is believed that it was Rocco and his crew who overpowered the rookie, took his gun, and handcuffed him to the telephone pole over there," he said, pointing to a telephone pole next to the alley, "with the rookie's own handcuffs."

"I read about the incident in the newspaper," Stone said. "I'll take care of it," she said, with a forced smile as she exited the vehicle. "Besides, if I need your help, you'll be right here to cover my back."

As Detective Stone walked toward the alley, Tom watched her. "Mar-done, what a nice ass on her. Hey, Verde, you banging her?"

"No. We just started working together. And besides, I don't think she likes me."

"Just you, or all men?" Mark said. "Word is that she's AC-DC, a switch hitter, if you catch my drift?"

"I don't believe that's true, Verde said. "It's just a rumor."

"Be ready to move," Tom said. "Rocco's always wired, a speed freak. He wouldn't give a second thought about fuckin' up a woman, especially a statie."

Verde looked back at Tom and smiled. "I saw Stone in action at the State Police Training Academy instructing the recruits on hand-to-hand combat. Five bucks says that if Rocco or his crew tries to overpower her, she'll kick the shit out of all of them."

"You're on, Verde, five bucks. Just be ready to help her."

Rocco was sitting on the concrete stairs in front of the apartment building. As he saw Stone walking toward him, he smiled a sadistic grin, lit up a Kool cigarette, and stood up.

Rocco was tall with a thin but wiry muscular frame. He wore a black sleeveless T-shirt with "Grand Funk Railroad" on the front in gold lettering. His jet-black hair was slicked back in a pompadour style resembling the teen idol Fabian. Around his neck was a thick gold rope chain with the Italian symbols of a malocchio, and an inverted horned hand. On the top of his well-defined upper right bicep was a tattoo with his first name and a decorative scroll underneath.

Detective Stone walked up to Rocco. Immediately, he noticed the gun partially exposed in her waistband.

"I'm looking for Freddie," she said, without expressing any sign of emotion as she looked at the other men who were approaching her.

"Don't know anyone here by that name, sweetheart," he said, smiling to the other men.

"Maybe I'll just take a look inside and see for myself," Stone said as she began to walk down the alley.

"You got a warrant?" Rocco said, blocking her path.

"Hey, Rocco," one of his crew said. "You know who this cunt is? She's the Ice Princess!"

"No shit!" he said, taking a long drag from his cigarette. "Maybe you and I can go inside and look for this Freddie guy, and after I give you some of this," he said, grabbing his crotch, "you won't be a fuckin' dike anymore," he said as his crew laughed.

"You have a filthy mouth, Mister Assenzi. Now step aside."

Rocco motioned with his eyes for his crew to circle her, which did not escape her notice.

"Oh shit," Mark said. "They're makin' their move. Let's go."

"Wait," Verde said. "Let's see where this goes."

One of the men tried to reach inside her jacket for her gun. She grabbed his wrist, twisting it backward with such force that it snapped before he fell to the ground, screaming. Rocco swung his arm around, trying to strike her in the face. She ducked and hit him with a short, straight, closed fist to his solar plexus, knocking the wind out of him. Then she hit him with her open hand to the bridge of his nose. Immediately, Rocco fell to his knees as torrents of blood spurted from his nose. The third man tried to rush her, but she motioned for him to stay put, and he decided that he didn't want any part of it.

Detective Stone drew her gun. "Get down on your knees, now," she commanded, "and place your hands behind your head!"

Rocco was rolling on the ground still trying to catch his breath. "You broke my nose, you fuckin' bitch."

Verde, Mark, and Tom exited the vehicle and began walking slowly toward Stone. She noticed that they didn't seem to be in any particular hurry. They were laughing and joking, and Tom was mimicking the blow that she had delivered to Rocco.

Tom reached into his pocket and handed Verde a five-dollar bill. "Mar-done, you were right, Verde. She's a fuckin' pitbull! It was worth the five dollars to see her kick the shit out of Rocco."

As they approached Stone, she turned toward them, seemingly annoyed. "Thanks for the assistance."

"We could see you had everything in control," Verde said as Mark and Tom nodded their heads in agreement like bobblehead dolls.

Mark leaned over to get a better look at Rocco's injuries. "Looks like it's broken, Rocco. No more pretty boy now! Hey, tough guy, what are the wise guys gonna think when they find out that you let a broad kick the shit out of you and break your nose?"

"Yeah, what are the wise guys gonna think?" Tom repeated.

"I'll tell you what they gonna think," Mark said. "That you're a pussy."

"Fuck you!" Rocco shouted, holding his hand over his nose. "And fuck her too!"

"I think you got it backward, Assenzi," Verde said. You're the one who's fucked. We all witnessed you and your men attempting to assault a state police detective."

"I don't want to press charges," Stone said, "unless Rocco has something he wants to press. I don't want to deal with the paperwork, and besides, I think he's learned his lesson for today, and we have bigger fish to fry."

Detective Stone walked up to the man who was still kneeling with his hands behind his head. When she came close to him, he put his arms around his face, believing she was going to strike him. "Relax," she said. "Are you going to tell me where Freddie is now?"

"He's where he is every afternoon," he said nervously, "at the Gemini Lounge."

The rescue squad arrived, along with several Providence Police vehicles. The EMTs got out quickly and helped Rocco up on a gurney. Stone got into Verde's vehicle and pulled it behind the rescue squad. Then she got out to talk with the responding officers.

"We'll take care of the paperwork at the station, Stone," Tom said. "You and Verde go see the Kook. Hey, Verde, I think you should let Stone interrogate the Kook. Mar-done, she'll terrorize him."

"It's been truly a pleasure working with you, Detective Stone," Mark said. "I wouldn't have missed it for the world."

Stone rolled her eyes and got back into the vehicle. As the EMT's were placing Rocco into the back of the rescue squad, he propped himself up and spit blood in her direction. "Payback's a bitch, you fuckin' dike!"

Verde got into the passenger side of his vehicle. As they pulled away, Stone smiled and waved good-bye to Rocco, which infuriated him even more. As the EMTs were closing the doors of the rescue squad, all you could hear was Rocco screaming obscenities.

Freddie the Kook

As they pulled up to the side of the Gemini Lounge, Stone spotted a dark-tan unmarked Providence Police vehicle. Captain Louis Lazarus was just getting out of his vehicle, but when he spotted Verde, he got back in, waved, and then sped off quickly.

"What was that all about?" Stone asked as she parked the car.

Verde looked at Stone, raising his eyebrows. "Louis was probably here to collect his monthly payment."

"If you know for sure that he's a dirty cop, why haven't internal affairs or the bureau investigated him? Why does he get a free pass?"

"A certain amount of corruption is unfortunately necessary, expected, and overlooked. Yes, he's in bed and shaking down the criminals. He knows all the players, and occasionally he uses them as informants, and without that relationship he would never have privy to the intel. He passes it along to your department as well as us. It's an unethical relationship, but it's productive."

"I wouldn't overlook his activities."

"Believe me; one day you will, and your superiors will order you to look the other way."

■■
The Gemini Lounge/Hotel was a sleazy establishment frequented by the dregs of society. Drug dealers, pimps, prostitutes, bookies, and mob associates hung out there on a daily basis. The brown brick-and-wood four-story building was in a rundown section on the outskirts of the mean streets just a stone's throw away from Bonded Vault.

Verde and Stone entered the dimly lit barroom and immediately drew the attention of the bartender and several of the patrons. The decorum of the barroom was outdated. Framed pictures of sports figures, some of them long deceased, and photographs of Italian singers like Dean Martin and Frank Sinatra adorned the dark and dusty paneling on the walls. A barely audible song by Italian crooner Louis Prima was playing on an outdated sound system.

A few patrons were sitting on tall barstools at a long oak bar. Several overly made-up prostitutes were hovering over their potential customers.

Verde spotted Freddie the Kook walking down a dark wooden stairway that led upstairs to the rooms that were rented by the hour. Tina, a petite but pretty Puerto Rican prostitute, was walking next to him. Freddie was talking to Tina, with a long cigarette in one hand and a glass of whiskey in the other and didn't notice that Verde was standing at the bottom of the stairs.

The Kook was a short man in his late fifties. His graying hair was disheveled. He was wearing a polyester jacket and a pair of pants that did not match the jacket. All his attire was wrinkled and dingy as if he wore that same outfit every day without cleaning or pressing them. He had a crooked satiated grin on his face, which quickly disappeared when he spotted Verde. He stopped walking and froze in midstride. The joy and color drained from his face, and his expression changed to one of trepidation. He regained his composure and continued down the stairs.

"You can go now, Tina," Freddie said. "See you next week." Freddie waited until she was out of hearing distance before he began talking to Verde. "You here to see me? I ain't got no beef with the feds."

"That's not what we have been hearing, Freddie. This is Detective Stone with the state police. She thinks you've been up to no good. Let's get a booth, and I'll tell you why we're here."

They sat down in a booth, Freddie against the wall so he could see who was entering and leaving. He didn't want anyone that knew him seeing that he was talking with the FBI.

"What's this all about?" Freddie asked. "I ain't done anything that the feds or the staties would be interested in. Sure, I'm selling questionable merchandise, but that's all. You know that, Verde."

"We'll see," Stone said, leaning toward Freddie in an attempt to intimidate him. "We're here about the Bonded Vault robbery. Reliable sources told us that you fenced some of the valuables from the heist. We want their names."

"Wow, there's nothing so refreshing as when a person is so candid and blunt," Verde said, with a touch of sarcasm. Stone couldn't determine at whom was he was directing his comment.

"What the fuck's going on here, Verde?" he asked in a voice slightly above a whisper. "Swear to God, I don't know nothing about the Vault. No one up the Hill does." He raised his right hand.

"You're going to tell us what you know, or you're going for a ride to the state police headquarters," Stone said, adamantly raising her voice, which caused several of the bar patrons to turn and look in their direction.

"Come on, Verde. Give me a break."

"You're talking with me now, not Verde," she said, with a cocky smile.

"She's right, Freddie. She may be here for Bonded Vault, but not me. That's not my case," he said, which drew an odd look from Stone.

"What's this, a double team?" Freddie asked. "Then what are you here for?"

"Dickie Callei."

Stone gave Verde another odd look. She had no idea what he was trying to accomplish.

Freddie leaned over and in a low, barely audible voice, pleaded with Verde. "How many years you know me, thirty? You want to get me whacked, is that it? You want me to end up in a shallow grave with a butcher's knife sticking out of my chest, like Dickie?"

"Don't give me that innocent look, Freddie," Verde said. "You must know who whacked Callei and if the Old Man ordered the hit."

"I swear on my mother's grave, I don't know nothing about who whacked Callei or the Vault."

"Freddie, Freddie, Freddie," Verde said, shaking his head. "Yes, we have known each other for over thirty years. Isn't your mother Anna the Geek? Isn't she still alive, and you're swearing on her grave?"

"I got carried away. It was just a figure of speech."

"I believe you, Freddie. And I guess if you really don't know anything, we're done here."

"I'm not through questioning this low life," Stone said, outraged.

"We're done here, Detective. Freddie knows better to lie to me. He knows the consequences. Don't you, Freddie?"

"I said," Stone said, raising her voice, "I'm not done questioning him!"

"You have to forgive Detective Stone, Freddie. She's a rookie...a little knew to this."

Stone was outraged, flabbergasted, and insulted by Verde's remark. Her face flushed red with anger, but she remained silent.

"See you later, Freddie," Verde said, getting up to leave.

Freddie was breathing a sigh of relief. Verde turned and paused and looked up at the ceiling as if he had just remembered something. On second thought, maybe we'll have to take you downtown to my office for questioning."

"I told you, I don't know anything."

"Yeah, yeah, yeah, on your mother's grave. I know I shouldn't tell you this, Freddie, but I'm going to come clean with you. An informant told us that Dickie was shaking you down and that he and Twitch were slapping you around. That's more than a motive. Maybe you had your nephew, Rocco, whack him. He's quite capable of shooting him five times and then sticking a kitchen knife in his chest."

"Bullshit! Yeah, Dickie was shakin' me down. The cops and the wise guys are always shakin' me down. You know how it works up here. It's the cost of doing business. Nothin' to whack someone over."

"You'll still have to come with us. I think you're not telling us everything you know."

"Wait a minute," Freddie said, smiling as if he was about to reveal something important. "If I give Stone something on the other thing, you know, Bonded Vault, will you let me slide on the other thing?"

Verde sat back down. "Maybe. It depends if your story pans out."

"What is it that you think you know?" Stone asked, doubting what the Kook was about to say.

Freddie looked around to make sure no one was listening. "Two days after the robbery, Mister C. went on a trip back to the Old Country.

He took a flight out of Logan to Milan and then to Switzerland and then to the Cayman Islands." He took along three suitcases in addition to his luggage."

"And you want a free pass for that?" Stone asked. "You expect us to believe that? How could you possibly know that?"

"My gumatta is best friends with his gumatta."

"Gumatta?" Stone asked, as she was unfamiliar with the term.

"A gumatta," Verde said, "is the girlfriend of a married Italian man."

"Yeah, that right," Freddie said. "Mister C. took his gumatta with him. She stayed at the hotel while Mister C. took the suitcases to someone in Milan. He returned to the hotel without the suitcases. A couple of days later they went to a bank in Switzerland and then spent a week in the Cayman Islands. Before they left they went to the Central Bank of Cayman. Are we square, Verde?"

"Yes," Verde said, shaking his head.

"If you tell anyone that I told you this, I'm a dead man."

"If we find out you made up this story," Stone said, "we'll be back to see you in Decatur Square."

"If I'm not there, I have to warn you about my nephew, Rocco. He's Ou-bots."

"Ou-bots?" Stone said, with an odd look on her face.

"Crazy," Freddie said, spinning his finger around his head in a circular motion. "I don't know where he gets it from."

"Let me get this straight," Stone said. "Rocco, your nephew, is a crazy psychopath. You're Freddie the *Kook*, and your mother is Anna the *Geek*. I'd say it runs in the family."

"Another ballbuster," Freddie said. "Verde, are we done?"

"Just about, but I wouldn't worry about Rocco. Right about now," Verde said, looking at his wristwatch, "Rocco is in the accident room getting his broken nose fixed."

"What the fuck happened?"

"He was, let us say, not too polite to Detective Stone, and she gave him an attitude adjustment. We're done here, Freddie, and for your sake, that information better not be bullshit."

When Verde and Stone got back into the vehicle, she didn't turn on the ignition. She had controlled her anger when he insulted her in front of the Kook, but she wasn't going to let him get away with what he had said.

"What the hell was that in there? I'm a rookie! New to this! If you think you're going to belittle me in front of that low life and marginalize my contributions to this investigation," she said, pushing her finger into his side, "you've got another thing coming, Mister FBI Special Agent. You can kiss my ass!"

Verde had a vivid image of what Stone just said. "That wouldn't be too unpleasant a request," he said in jest, which outraged her all the more.

"What do you mean by that?"

"Kissing your ass," he said, joking once again.

"What!"

"Lighten up. Calm down. I was just playing you. And besides, I like my nose exactly the way it is," he said, looking in the rearview mirror. I think it went well in there." He tried changing the subject in an attempt to calm her down.

"And that's your justification for what you told that idiot about me? Now I know what everyone has said about you is right on the money."

"And that is?"

"That you're an asshole. An arrogant, self-absorbed, egotistical son of a bitch with an overinflated opinion of your self-worth and importance!"

Verde smiled. "Maybe you'll tell me what they say are my bad qualities?" he asked jokingly. "I know someone else *they* say has many of the same qualities."

"Who?" she asked, believing he was about to say her.

Verde lowered the visor in front of Stone. "Just look in the mirror."

"I don't think so!"

"If we're going to work together, we're going to have to work...together. That's why I chose you."

"You chose me?"

Colonel Stone asked me who I wanted to work with me as a liaison between the FBI and the state police on this case."

"Really? Thanks for the privilege," she said sarcastically. Then she thought for a moment, and a look of skepticism appeared on her face. "Oh, now I understand. I've heard of your reputation with the opposite sex. What did you think? You'd dazzle me with your *charming* personality, bat your big blue eyes, and we'd end up in bed?"

"Don't flatter yourself. From what I've heard about your reputation, Ice Princess, your last name, Stone, suits your personality to a T."

"Then I guess the next question is why. Why me?"

"I read your file."

"You read my file! My file!"

"That's right. Let's start with your first name. It isn't Rose, it's Rosetta. Your name is Rosetta Stone," Verde said, smiling. "What were your parents thinking about?"

"I was named after my grandmother. Do you have a problem with that?"

"Not if you don't," he said, with a snicker.

Stone had no response, and Verde could tell that she was displeased by his revelation. "What else have you gathered about me?"

"You're a competent detective, and it's obvious you can handle yourself on the street. But you're in the big league now, in the big game, and that's just not enough."

"And you're going to be, what, my tutor? I've done quite well without you, and furthermore," she said growing angry, "what did you mean by, 'it's just not enough'?"

"You could be a better investigator than I ever was or will be. However, what you lack I possess, and vice versa."

"How so?" she asked, squinting her eyes and shaking her head at what he just said. "I can't wait to hear this."

"You're more of an intellectual than I am, and a creative thinker. I saw your test scores at the academy. You tested off the charts. However, that may be your undoing."

"What, I'm overqualified for this job?"

"No. You grew up in the rich suburbs in Barrington. Your parents were both professionals. You attended private schools...Ivy League college. Graduated top in your class."

"Someone's been prying into my background. And all these things are a disadvantage? You sound jealous."

"I grew up in the gutter, so to speak, with the same type of criminal element we're investigating. My education was not from the Ivy League but the school of hard knocks on the mean streets of Providence. You are, and I hate to admit it, more intelligent than I am. You're bookwise, not streetwise. You think you are, but you're not. That's why we'd make a great team. What I lack you possess, and what you lack I possess."

Stone thought for a moment. Now she despised him even more. Her pride would not let her acknowledge that he was probably right. But she wanted to defend herself. "Let me get this right. What you're saying is that I'm not up to the task."

"You're not," Verde said, smiling.

"Okay, Mr. Know It All, tell me why."

"You didn't comprehend how I was playing Freddie. Although the Kook is not a rocket scientist, he could see the good-cop, bad-cop routine a mile away. He's seen it many times before. I was playing him with misdirection with the Dickie Callei angle, and you couldn't see the play. You were too straightforward with your interrogation. Any criminal could see where you were going and what you were after. Yes, the Kook is an idiot, but one day you're going to run into criminals who are as smart as you are and maybe a few even smarter."

"Yeah, like who?"

"You met one today and didn't even know it. Remy Gerard, a.k.a. the Frenchman. Don't ever underestimate him. The Frenchman is a master criminal. In school, until he quit, he was in the top of his class. If anyone up here could have planned and carried out the Vault robbery, my bet is that it was Remy."

Verde could see that Stone had calmed down, digesting and analyzing what he was saying.

"I knew what you were doing, but you didn't have to belittle me in the process."

"Yes, I did. It was part of the play, and you didn't play your part. Didn't the end justify the means? We got a big piece of one thing we came here to find out."

"Really? We really didn't find out anything that the FBI and state police hadn't already surmised."

Verde shook his head. "After I finish writing the report, I forward a copy to the colonel, my headquarters, and the Providence Police. It will state that a reliable informant confirmed that Raymond Patriarca sanctioned the Bonded Vault robbery. Then he had his trusted courier, Mr. Caruso, a.k.a. Freddie C., liquidate his share of the heist with a mob fence in Milan and then launder the proceeds in a Swiss bank and in the Cayman Islands. Before I write the report, I'll assign a few agents to work with Interpol to confirm Freddie C.'s movements to verify the Kook's story. Even though we got that information, it won't be enough to tie the Old Man to the robbery."

As Verde spoke, a call came in on his car phone. He talked briefly, hung up the phone, and smiled. "We just got a very big break in the case. One of my agents just finished an interview with a Barbara Oliver, an employee at Bonded Vault. She gave a statement and positively identified the lead gunman in the heist. I know who he is. He's from Massachusetts;

Robert 'The Duce' Dussault. We'll go back to my office and issue an APB, and I'll get an arrest warrant out for him."

Detective Stone was pleased with the news, and for the first time all day, a genuine smile appeared on her face. She had accepted Verde's explanation of the incident with the Kook with reservations but still didn't approve the role he made her play. She knew she had learned something valuable that day. She saw Verde's thought process and just how deceitful and cunning he could be to get the desired result. However, she also recognized how adept he had been in extracting the information from the Kook, and she began to wonder if he had just placated and played her the same way. For the time being, she would take him at his word, and keep him on a short leash, a very short leash.

The Duce Is Wild in Vegas

Oh, the shark, babe,

Has such teeth, dear,

And he shows them

Pearly white.

Just a jack knife has

Old Mac Heath, babe,

And he keeps it

Out of sight.

—Weill and Brecht,

"The Ballad of Mack the Knife"

8:20 p.m., Las Vegas

When Dussault, Floyd, and his girlfriend arrived in Las Vegas, they stared out of the taxi windows, mesmerized by the thousands of colorful flashing neon lights. They were taken to the luxurious MGM Grand Hotel Casino. Floyd had procured perfect fake IDs for everyone, and they checked into one of the best suites under their new assumed names. Dussault's new name was Dennis Allen. Chucky's girlfriend asked the Duce why he booked such an expensive suite. He told her that he was going to go first class as long as his money, luck, and freedom would last.

A well-dressed bell hop took their luggage up to their suite. He was a clean-cut, polished young man in his early thirties, although he looked much younger, like a recent college graduate. Floyd's girlfriend entered the room and began unpacking their luggage.

Chucky and Dussault stayed in the hallway to talk with the bellhop.

"I'm Paul Purcello," the bellhop said, shaking both men's hands. "Everyone in Vegas calls me Paulie."

Purcello determined by their attire, the way they carried themselves, and the expensive suite that these men were high rollers. In Vegas they called men like them "whales," who had vast sums of money to spend on their extravagances. With his "unique" talent for getting these types of patrons anything they desired, he made a small fortune plying their vices. After all, this was Vegas, Sin City, and if you had the cash, a man like Purcello could make all your desires and wildest fantasies come true.

As Paulie talked with them, Dussault began to feel uneasy. Although he was speaking to both men, he kept staring at the Duce. Finally, Dussault looked directly into Paulie's eyes with a glaring stare. "Do you know me?" he asked, with a stern voice.

"Excuse me for staring, Mr. Allen, but did anyone ever tell you that you're a dead ringer for the late singer Bobby Darin?"

Chucky and Dussault looked at each other and laughed.

"He stayed here often when he performed. I tell you, the resemblance is uncanny. There's a show at the Dunes Casino with a Bobby Darin impersonator who sings all of his hits spot-on, but you look a lot more like Darin than he does. If you desire, I can get you front-row tickets to the show as well as all the best shows in Vegas: Sinatra, Tom Jones, Siegfried and Roy."

"That's sounds great," Chucky said. "Mr. Darin and I will let you know what shows we want to see," he said as they all laughed.

"I double here at the MGM as your, let's say, concierge. Anything you need, and I mean anything, I'm your man."

"What do you mean by anything?" Dussault asked.

"You name it, and I'll get it. Grass, coke, uppers, downers, call girls. Anything and everything you desire."

"I'm all set with a woman," Chucky said, "but my friend here, he's in the market for a woman."

"That's my specialty; showgirl-quality women, clean, beautiful, and discrete, and they'll do anything for a price."

"Anything?" the Duce asked, with a devilish grin.

"You name it, and they'll do it."

"I'm looking for a woman just like that, but more of a long-term companion, for let's say a month."

"I have just the woman in mind, and she's a knockout. Just give me the word, and I'll send her up to see you."

"Fine," Dussault said. "Send her up. The sooner the better."

"We also want you to locate a late-model luxury vehicle," Chucky said.

"I'll get to it right away," Purcello said.

As he was leaving, Dussault peeled off a fifty-dollar bill from a two-inch roll of bills, which did not escape Paulie's notice.

"Thank you, gentlemen," he said, stuffing the bill in his pocket. "And remember, anything you need, twenty-four seven."

Chucky and Duce went into their room, and they both took a shower and relaxed. About an hour later, Paulie returned and gave Chucky the keys to a silver Lincoln Continental Mark Four.

"Wow," Duce said. "That was quick."

Paulie just smiled and left.

That evening Dussault and Floyd dressed in custom three-piece suits. Chucky's girlfriend wore a black evening dress, a string of pearls, and the engagement ring he had given her earlier, along with a dozen long-stem roses. They dined on prime rib and lobsters and drank two bottles of Dom Perignon. Then they went to the MGM Casino for an evening of gambling. Chucky was a degenerate gambler, sometimes betting a thousand dollars on a single roll of the dice. Occasionally, he would send his girlfriend to the front desk to get more cash from their safety deposit box.

The Duce had played craps all his life. He honed his skills at first on the back alleys in Massachusetts, rolling dice for a quarter to make point. When he was older, he played in prison and in illegal mob gambling establishments. After a short while, Floyd had lost thousands of dollars, which gave his girlfriend reason for concern. However, Dussault was up nearly $4,000. He retired for the evening, leaving Chucky and his girlfriend still playing dice.

The Duce entered his suite, took off his tie and jacket, and made himself bourbon on ice in a square monogrammed MGM glass. There came a series of soft knocks at his door. When he opened it up, he was pleasantly surprised.

"Mr. Allen," she said, with a soft voice that purred like a kitten, "Paul Purcello sent me. I'm Kayla Spelling."

Dussault was captivated by the vision before him and the fragrant smell of her floral-scented perfume. She was beautiful, sexy, and the top of her breasts were slightly exposed through her tightly fitting beige chiffon dress. She wore very little makeup, and her lightly tanned complexion was perfect, like that of a fashion model. She wore her dark-blond hair in an updo, as if she was going out for a special occasion. Duce thought to himself that she looked like a combination of the movie stars Stella Stevens and a young Angie Dickinson.

Dussault made her a drink, and they sat down on the edge of his bed.

"Purcello told me that you were interested in a long-term companion for your stay in Las Vegas. I have to ask up front for how long you would like this arrangement and what the financial consideration will be."

"Would twenty-five hundred a week, plus all expenses, for about a month or so do?"

Kayla took a sip of her drink and nodded yes with a wide smile. "Would you like me to undress now?" she said, unclasping the back of her dress. "After all, you'll want to see that you're getting your money's worth." They both laughed.

The Duce nodded. "I guess this is where the expression 'It'll be my pleasure,' comes from."

Kayla undressed slowly, teasing Dussault, and placed her clothing and undergarments neatly on a nightstand next to the bed. Her body was flawless, and her natural breasts were those of a younger woman, with large, darkly colored areola and pointed nipples. When she was naked, she began undressing him, removing his clothing and placing them next to hers. By the time she had removed all his clothing, he was fully erect. She positioned him on the edge of the bed and performed oral sex on him, moving her lips and tongue slowly to prolong and heighten his carnal pleasure. After he reached orgasm, they laid on the bed, facing each other. A short while later, he was fully erect again. He positioned her on the edge of the bed, extending her legs on the side of his head, caressing her sleek thighs and the lean, sinewy muscles on her legs and lightly tanned calves. She reached down to help him guide his manhood deeply into her. At first Dussault moved slowly. Then as he was reaching orgasm, he quickened his pace, and she gyrated her hips to accentuate his pleasure.

They took a shower together and dressed for a nightcap at the downstairs nightclub. A man in a white tuxedo was playing soft, slow tunes on a grand piano. The rest of the evening was spent on idle talk and about some of the places the Duce had planned for them to visit in the following weeks.

The next morning, Dassault thought it would be nice touch to impress his new companion, so he asked Paulie to have a limousine pick up Kayla at her apartment after she had packed a few suitcases for her extended stay with him.

In the days that followed, the Duce made sure he got the "biggest bang for his buck" in his arrangement with Kayla. They had sex several times each day. She couldn't remember a man who had such a sexual appetite and endurance as Dussault, and she told him so, which pleased his ego.

Dussault was enjoying and becoming accustomed to living the lifestyle of a high roller, even if it was built upon a lie and stolen money. He lavished Kayla with an expensive wardrobe and purchased jewelry for her and himself from the Gold Rush, a mob-owned-and-operated pawn shop just off the main strip.

On their first Saturday night in Las Vegas, they were going to the Dunes Casino to see the show featuring the Bobby Darin impersonator. Everyone in their entourage dressed in their finest attire, and a limousine drove them to the show.

When they arrived, they were escorted to the foyer of the amphitheater and waited for the doors to open. As the crowd began to form, several elderly couples gathered near their party. They were typical Las Vegas tourists. The men were dressed in polyester leisure suits and out-of-date checkered and iridescent suits. The women wore pantsuits and had teased, blown up hairstyles with ample amounts of hairspray and overly done makeup. They clutched onto their programs, waving them about as they talked loudly about the places they visited in Las Vegas.

One of the women in the group pointed to the Duce and nudged one of the other women to come with her. She opened her oversized pocketbook, took out a pen, and walked up to Dussault.

"Excuse me, Mr. Darin," she said sheepishly. "May I have your autograph?" She handed him the program and her pen.

Everyone in Dussault's party laughed. The Duce looked at Kayla and could see she was surprised and impressed that someone would think that her date was a celebrity.

"I'm very sorry, ma'am," Dussault said in an apologetic tone, "but I'm not Bobby Darin."

The woman apologized to Dussault, and she and her friend walked back to their group, occasionally looking back at the Duce.

"I guess Paulie was right," Chucky said. "You must really resemble Darin."

Several ushers in tuxedos opened the doors and escorted them to their seats in an exclusive section of the amphitheater. They sat down on plush clamshell leather seats in the front row. The Duce could see that Kayla was impressed by their front-row accommodations. In all her years living in Las Vegas, she had not been accustomed to this type of preferential treatment.

The show started with a comic who told off-color jokes laced with profanity. Next, seminude Vegas showgirls performed several dance numbers. After a short intermission, the showgirls reentered to introduce the Bobby Darin impersonator, accompanied by a full orchestra. He sounded just like the deceased crooner and performed all of his hit tunes including, "By the Sea" and "Dream Lover," and ended with his signature song, "Mack the Knife."

***

After the show, Chucky went back to the MGM to play craps. Dussault and Kayla walked down the strip to Binion's Horseshoe Casino so he could play high-stakes poker. There were dozens of round tables in the smoke-filled main gambling room featuring high-stakes poker games. The walls were decorated with tacky red velvet wallpaper with the diamond Binion's logo printed throughout. Elevated at the end of the room was a Plexiglas cube with $1 million in cash stacked in the shape of a pyramid, with one security guard standing on each side.

Dussault went to the cashier and purchased a few thousand dollars in chips. Then he stood and watched one of the tables consisting of five men and two women and a house dealer.

The Duce was a seasoned gambler. He was very good at craps, but his real forte was poker. He stood at a distance, watching the players and trying to determine their level of play and their tells. Most players had a tell, a small nuance, a repeated gesture that a seasoned player like Dussault could use to determine the strength and weakness of a player's hand, how they bet in a given situation, and when they were bluffing. He knew by his observations that with any luck and his skill, he was going to clean house at that table. Before he sat down to play, he formulated a strategy. He would take their money slowly but steadily, occasionally "dumping' a hand to make the other players feel that they had a chance of beating him, and that he was just another "poker stiff' and not a card shark. Little did he know at the time that his ability to read the nuances of an opponent would soon be the difference between life and a very violent death.

One of the players tapped out, and the Duce sat down to play. Kayla sat down a short distance away at the bar and ordered a rum and Coke as she watched her man play.

The ante at the table was $200 per hand, and the house took $100 from each hand dealt. The house dealer moved a Plexiglas pyramid in front of each player when it was their turn to name the type of poker played. Dussault thought it ironically appropriate that when it was his turn to name his type of poker game, he called out seven-card stud with deuces wild.

After playing for nearly two hours, Dussault was up a little over four thousand. Every now and then, he would take a small stack of one-hundred-dollar chips and put them discretely into his pocket. He didn't want the other players at the table to see that he was taking so much of their money. He turned toward Kayla, and she smiled, knowing that he was winning, but the Duce could see that she looked bored. He thanked the other players and tipped the dealer with a fifty-dollar chip, and he left the table. As they walked to the cashier, Kayla leaned over and gave him a soft kiss. She knew he was winning, but she didn't know how much until he took a stack of chips from each of his jacket pockets. He gave her five one-hundred-dollar chips for her to cash in and keep the proceeds. She stood by him, arm in arm, as the cashier counted out his winnings in large denomination bills.

It had been warmer than usual for a November night in Las Vegas. The Duce and Kayla took a late-night dip in the Olympic-size outdoor pool at the MGM Grand before retiring to their suite. Kayla expressed her gratitude to her new man for sharing his winnings with her by giving him an extended marathon of sex.

***

After a few weeks, Chucky had burned through tens of thousands of dollars gambling. On the contrary, Dussault had more money than when he arrived in Las Vegas. Chucky's fiancée did not want him losing any more money and convinced him to return to Rhode Island. Chucky and Dussault said their good-byes, leaving the "love birds," as Floyd put it, on their own.

After Chucky left, Dussault and Kayla decided to take a trip to the West Coast by car and see the sights along the way. There was no longer a need for the Duce to keep his expensive suite at the MGM Hotel. Kayla proposed that Dussault move in with her at her apartment off the main strip. He agreed to pick up the rent while he was staying there. She told him that it was not necessary, that they were now like girlfriend and boyfriend, but the Duce insisted on paying his own way.

Kayla drove toward the West Coast in the silver Lincoln Continental Mark Four because Dussault never learned how to drive. Midway on their trip, Kayla began teaching him.

When they arrived in San Francisco, they took snapshots on a high cliff overlooking the Golden Gate Bridge. They spent several days in Disneyland. The Duce felt alive and enthusiastic, like a little boy, as Kayla and he smashed each other on the bumper-car ride. They walked down the midway hand in hand, eating funnel cakes and kettle corn. The Duce felt like he was on his honeymoon rather than having a relationship between a jon and a call girl.

They traveled to Hollywood and checked into the luxurious Beverly Hills Hilton Hotel. On several afternoons they strolled down Rodeo Drive, where Dussault lavished Kayla with expensive clothing and jewelry.

The Duce was happier now than he had ever been in his life. He had plenty of money, more money from the heist to come, and a beautiful and sexy woman at his side. He felt that he had finally met the women of his dreams. Maybe, he thought, he could buy investment income-producing property, settle down with Kayla, and have a normal, stable life far away from his life of crime and uncertainty. Looming in the back of his mind was the thought that he was a fugitive from justice and that the dreams for his future were on borrowed time and could end at any moment.

On their last day at the Hilton, they were relaxing poolside at their private, drapery-enclosed cabana. Dussault lay on a lounge chair wearing a plaid boxer-type bathing suit and a pair of brown teardrop sunglasses. Kayla had just come out from a swim in the pool, and he handed her a large monogrammed hotel towel to dry off as he admired her sleek, shapely body.

As she brushed back her wet hair, she leaned over and gave him a kiss and then sat back on her lounge chair. "Dennis, what do you do for a living?"

"What do you think I do for a living?"

"I don't know, maybe a businessman or you're independently wealthy."

The Duce gave her a soft pat on her backside and raised up his sunglasses. "I'm a criminal," he said matter-of-factly, without emotion or inflection in his voice.

"Quit joking," she said, with a half smile, not knowing if he was being serious.

"I am being serious. I'm a lifelong criminal."

"What type of criminal?" she asked, still thinking he was putting her on.

"High-end heists, all well-planned robberies, nothing small, nothing violent."

She still thought he was joking. "Really?" she asked, sitting up.

"I'm leveling with you. I trust you, and it's only fair that you know. Do you have a problem with my vocation?"

"No," she said, after remaining silent for a few moments as she tried to absorb and understand the nature of what he had just revealed. "I had a feeling it might be something like that." She looked off in the distance. "Actually, I've led most of my life on the fringes of the law. In many ways, I'm just like you."

The Duce smiled. He now knew that she had accepted him for what he really was as sort of a kindred spirit. "Then I guess you could say we were made for each other," he said, giving her a peck, and she reciprocated with a hug and a long, passionate kiss.

They ate dinner at the finest restaurant in Beverly Hills, checked out of the hotel, and returned to Las Vegas.

Blood in the Water

Plots, true and false
Are necessary things,
To raise up commonwealth,
And ruin kings.

— John Dryden

Agent Verde arrived early at the Providence office of the FBI's Organized Crime Task Force. He had already put into action the first part of his plan to turn up the heat and flush out Dussault. On the day before, he released information to the local newspapers that stated an employee of the Bonded Vault Storage Facility, Barbara Oliver, had positively Identified Robert "The Duce" Dussault as the lead gunman in the Bonded Vault Heist.

Verde and Special Agent Paul Rodrigues had been rehearsing the script that Verde had written for the plan that would come to be known as Operation Blood in the Water.

"Where's Stone?" Rodrigues asked.

Verde sat back on his desk chair and placed his hands behind his head. A devious smile appeared on his face. "I sent her out to follow up on a lead."

"What lead?"

"She came in early and was feisty, fidgeting, pacing the room. She wanted to arrest someone or kick someone's ass. I don't know, maybe it's that time of the month," he said, shaking his head. "So I told her that a reliable informant said that Joey Onions may have some information about Bonded Vault. I sent her to Federal Hill to find him."

Rodrigues laughed. "You sent her to find small-time hood Joseph "Joey Onions" Scallion? You know the only way she's going to find him is with a Ouija board or at a séance. He's long gone, and they'll never find the body."

"It's a wild goose chase. I know that, but she didn't, but she soon will. I figured I'd rent some space in her head for busting my balls all morning."

"She's going to be fucking pissed when she comes in."

"Yeah, yeah, yeah, I know. Just don't laugh when she comes in, and play it straight."

Detective Stone entered the office wearing her usual matronly dark-green business suit. Her dark, short hair was pushed back into a tight, neat bun. She had a small paper bag in her hand with the name "Joey" printed on the outside with a bold black marker. Verde looked up, trying to keep a straight face. He gave her a smile, but it was more than a casual smile. She could sense his amorous expression. She had seen many men look at her with the same expression, and she didn't want to acknowledge or encourage what she perceived as an obvious flirtation.

He could sense that she was trying to conceal her outrage. Her faced was flushed red with anger.

"Good morning, Rose," Verde said nonchalantly. "I'd like to introduce you to Agent Rodrigues."

"Nice to finally meet you," Rodrigues said, standing up to shake her hand and trying to keep a straight face. Finally, he turned around and tried to suppress his laughter.

"You're both assholes!" she shouted. "And you, Verde, you're a son of a bitch."

"My, my, my, how out of character, Detective Stone," Verde said, with mock indignation, trying to suppress his laughter.

"You sent me to look for Joey Onions. I asked around like the dupe you made out of me. I didn't know why everyone up the Hill was giving me an odd look, and when I left, they were all laughing. Then I met a fruit peddler with a push cart and asked him for the whereabouts of Joey Onions. He laughed and said he was dead, executed, and since it was a mob hit, 'they'll never find the body,' he said. And when I asked him who else knew he was dead, he looked around to see if anyone was listening, smiled, and said, 'Everyone.' I told him you sent me out to find Joey Onions. Even he said that you're an asshole. Then he gave me this paper bag and said it was for you. Don't ever let it happen again!" she shouted, pushing her finger into his chest.

"It was a joke, a joke. Calm down."

Stone opened the paper bag and dumped the contents on Verde's desk. It was a large yellow onion. "Here's the only onion you find up the Hill!"

"If you've calmed down now, you've arrived just in time." Verde could see that her demeanor was returning to normal.

"Just in time for what, another joke? Stone asked defiantly.

"Operation Blood in the Water," Rodrigues said. "We're just about to implement the plan."

"And what is Operation Blood in the Water?" she asked.

"It's a red herring," Rodrigues said.

"A red herring?" she asked, squinting her eyes.

"A false narrative," Verde said. "Misinformation."

"Like me looking for Joey Onions."

"No," Rodrigues said as he flipped through the business section of a phone directory until he reached the section for attorneys. "How about DeAngelis?"

"No," Verde said. "He a good guy, and powerful. We don't want to fuck with him."

Rodrigues kept flipping through the pages. "How about Goldstein, Harold Goldstein?"

"Perfect," Verde said. "He's a headline grabber. He'll take the bait and be ecstatic to get his name in the papers connected to such a high-profile case."

"I know of him," Stone said. "He's an honest lawyer."

"An honest lawyer!" Verde said, looking over to Rodrigues. "That's an oxymoron."

"I still don't know what you're trying to accomplish?" Stone asked.

"You'll see right now," Rodrigues said as he dialed the number to Goldstein's office and then turned on the speaker phone.

Goldstein's secretary answered the phone.

"I'm Robert Dussault," Rodrigues said. "I was the lead gunman in the Bonded Vault robbery. There's an APB out for my arrest, and I'd like to turn myself into Goldstein."

The secretary put him on hold. Then Goldstein answered the phone. "How may I be of assistance to you, Mr. Dussault? My secretary briefed me on your situation, and I read the article about you in the newspaper this morning."

"I talked with an FBI agent in Providence. His name was Verde."

"Yes, I know Agent Verde. He's the director in charge of the FBI's Organized Crime Task Force in Rhode Island."

"I want you to coordinate a deal, a plea agreement before I turn myself in to you. I want the agreement in writing. I don't trust the feds."

"What were the conditions of the deal you were discussing with Agent Verde?"

"I told him in exchange for naming and testifying against all the other guys who robbed the Vault and the mobster who sanction the heist, I want immunity from prosecution, a new identity, entrance into the witness protection program, a house, and a job."

"And he agreed to those terms?"

"Yes, he did, but I don't trust him. That's why I want you to work out the deal with him...in writing."

"May I ask, who's the mobster you are going to name that sanctioned the robbery?"

"The numero uno, the big cheese, Raymond L. S. Partiarca."

"Oh, I see," Goldstein said, surprised.

"Even before I testify against the Old Man, he'll put out a contract out on my life. I'm willing to bet he already did. Mobsters are probably trying to find me after the article in the newspaper, as we speak."

"All right, Mr. Dussault. I'll contact Agent Verde and set up the deal. How can I contact you?"

"I'll contact you."

"I'll set it up right away. In the meantime, keep safe."

Rodrigues hung up the phone. "How was that?" he asked Verde, looking over his shoulder.

"Perfect."

"Is this legal?" Stone asked.

"Define legal?" Rodrigues asked rhetorically.

"A certain amount of deception is allowable in order to catch a criminal," Verde said. "We do it all the time. What would you have us do, place an ad in the newspaper and ask Dussault if he'd kindly turn himself in?"

Stone shook off his offhanded comment. "You know you've just placed a target on his back."

"The Duce did that the moment he pulled the heist. And it's not one target. It's actually four."

"Four? How do you come up with four?"

"Ours, the underworld guys he robbed, and the other men in his crew. They'll try to whack him before he can link them to the crime. And lastly, the Old Man. If Dussault testifies against him, he'll go back to prison. The minute this hits the newspapers, he'll put a contract out on his life. Sometimes, in order to catch a criminal like Dussault, you have to be more cunning and deceitful than he is. Once we put blood in the water, so to speak, the sharks will most certainly come."

"And then what?"

"We'll just have to hope," Rodrigues said, leaning back in his chair and placing his hands behind his head, "that he panics, slips up. Desperate men do desperate things. We'll just have to get to him before they do."

"Or maybe just after?" Stone asked.

Rodrigues didn't answer her. He just tipped his head as if to say, "If that's what it is, then that's what it is."

■■

A few days later, the front-page article in the *Providence Journal* gave the details of the agreement. It stated that in exchange for his testimony against the other men involved in the heist, Dussault would enter the government's witness protection program and receive immunity from prosecution. The article went on to say that Dussault also agreed to testify against a high-ranking member of the Mafia who sanctioned the robbery in exchange for his testimony. The high-ranking mafioso is alleged to be Raymond L. S. Patriarca.

> You know when the shark bites
> With his teeth, dear,
> Scarlet billows
> Start to spread.
> Fancy gloves though
> Wears Old Mac Heath, babe,
> So there's never
> Never a trace of red.

Marked for Death

December 3, 7:00 a.m.

The Old Man sat at a small round wooden table in his Atwells Avenue Coin-o-Matic office in Providence. A mob lackey made him his customary morning espresso with a shot of anisette and a lemon wedge on the side. He opened the morning newspaper and lit up an unfiltered cigarette. It dangled from his lips. As he read the front-page article, his anger grew.

LEAD GUNMAN IN BONDED VAULT ROBBERY COPS PLEA DEAL

Several days ago, Robert "The Duce" Dussault, who has been identified as the lead gunman in the Bonded Vault robbery, contacted Providence attorney Harold S. Goldstein to negotiate a plea agreement in exchange for his testimony in the multimillion-dollar heist. Goldstein confirmed that Dussault requested immunity from prosecution, entry into the federal witness protection program, and a new identity in exchange for his testimony. According to attorney Goldstein, Dussault will provide law enforcement authorities with the details and names of his accomplices in the robbery as well as the high-ranking member of the Mafia who authorized the heist. It has been alleged by an undisclosed source in the

Rhode Island State Police that the high-ranking mafioso is reputed to be Raymond L. S. Patriarca.

Estimates of the amount stolen in the heist run as high as $30 million, according to law enforcement authorities. The preliminary plea agreement has been confirmed by Attorney General Julius Michelson as well as Vincent J. Verde, Director of Rhode Island's FBI's Organized Crime Task Force. When asked for further details of the agreement or the whereabouts of Dussault, Verde stated that "the Bureau does not comment on ongoing investigations."

The Old Man read the newspaper article again and then flung it across the room. When Mister C. entered the Coin-O-Matic, he had already read the article and knew Ray would be infuriated. The Old Man put his finger to his lips, signaling Mister C. not to talk. They left by the back door and went for a walkabout along the back alleys of Atwells Avenue. Although the Old Man had the Coin-O-Matic swept for bugs every week, he didn't want to take the chance that the feds might be listening to what he was about to tell Mister C.

It was a brisk morning, and the Old Man turned up the collar on his brown jacket to keep warm. "You were there when I told Remy that I didn't want to spend another day in prison. What part of that didn't he understand? 'All stand-up guys,' he said. 'Guys that would never rat.'"

"I was there, Ray," Mister C. said. "I know what you told him."

"Well, you know what has to be done. You have the Frenchman come to see you. Not tomorrow, not tonight, now!" he said, pointing his finger toward the ground in defiance. "You make it clear. I don't care what it takes, how much it costs, or who does it. This chiacchierone, this Dussault, has to go, ASAP!"

"I'll get right on it, Ray."

An hour later, Mister C. had a similar conversation with the Frenchman. He gave Remy the Old Man's orders and asked him if he knew the whereabouts of Dussault. The Frenchman told him that Chucky Floyd told him the Duce had taken up with a hooker and was living at the MGM Grand Hotel under the name of Dennis Allen. Mister C. kept repeating the Old Man's urgency to whack Dussault ASAP.

In the FBI's office and in the state police headquarters, both Verde and Stone read the newspaper article. They surmised that the hierarchy of the mob had already put a plan in motion to have Dussault executed. Now the both hoped that they could get him before the mob did.

Mister C. called the Old Man's associates in Las Vegas to make discrete inquiries as to the exact location of the Duce. Bobby Amafitano, Pomi Vecchione, and Frank "Frankie Boy" Baletta had been sent to Las Vegas to oversee and protect the Old Man's interests in one of the casinos. One of their duties was to make sure none of the other wise guys from other "outfits" muscled in on the Old Man's action and to make sure the "skim" wasn't "skimmed" before the Old Man got his piece. Every few weeks one of them would come back to Providence with a valise stuffed with cash and deliver it to him.

All of Raymond's men were given nondescript jobs at the casino. When they spoke, which was seldom outside of their inner circle, it was with guttural accents as if they were from Brooklyn, New York, or Southern New Jersey. After several inquiries, they told Mister C. that Dussault had checked out of the MGM Hotel and was living with a call girl and gave him her address and telephone number.

*

Dussault awoke early as usual. He had planned a leisure day of sightseeing and gambling. He put on his pants and T-shirt and looked over at Kayla, who was still sleeping. Kayla slept in the nude. Every morning they would awake intertwined with one of his hands caressing the soft rise of her belly and the other tucked in between her breasts. He went into the kitchen and made a pot of coffee. Kayla's small apartment was quaint and cozy and neatly kept. Every room of the apartment was adorned with asparagus ferns, Christmas cactus, and assorted flowering perennials.

The phone rang in the bedroom. Dussault wondered who would be calling this early in the morning. Kayla awoke, stood up, and stretched. Her milky white breasts and midsection contrasted the tanned outline of the bathing suit she had been wearing in California. She slipped into a pink terrycloth mini bathrobe and tied the sash around her midsection.

As the Duce picked up the phone, she sat on the edge of the bed and listened to the conversation. She soon came to realize that the other person on the line was Chucky Floyd. She could see a strange metamorphosis taking place, a side of Dussault she had never seen before. The change was fueled by his growing sense of paranoia and partially from all of the "obies," which were powerful amphetamines that resembled speckled breath mints, that the Duce had been popping like M&M's the night before. The first thing that made him suspicious was how he knew he was staying with Kayla and how he got her telephone number and by what he was telling him.

"We gotta straighten this thing out," Chucky said, with a sense of nervousness and urgency in his voice.

"What thing?" Dussault asked, bewildered.

"There's a story in the newspaper that identified you as the lead gunman in the heist. A witness gave a positive ID. The story says that you contacted a Jew lawyer and the feds. The article said you want to cut a deal to testify against all of us, including the Old Man."

"Bullshit!" Dussault exclaimed. "I never ratted out anyone, and I never will. I never talked with the feds or that lawyer. The story's a plant. Someone is playing all of you like dupes. It's a setup."

"I told them that. That it was a set up. That's why they asked me to straighten this thing out. You know me, Duce. I'm your best friend. Your very best friend."

The more Chucky kept repeating and emphasizing that he was his best friend, the more paranoid the Duce became. He now knew that he was living on borrowed time. The order had been given. He knew the mob usually would send a friend to put him as ease, someone he'd never suspect to whack him. He was marked for death.

"Is Kayla with you?" Chucky asked.

Dussault hesitated. "Yes, she is," he said, looking over his shoulder at her. She was still sitting on the edge of the bed wondering what he was talking about that would cause him to have these unfamiliar expressions on his face that was unlike anything she had seen before.

"Don't tell her you're talking to me."

The hair on the back of Dussault's neck tingled. "How stupid does he think I am?" he thought. "He doesn't want me to tell her who I'm talking to so when they whack me, she won't be able to tell the cops who was the last person I was talking to."

"I won't," the Duce said. "I won't tell her anything," he said, looking at Kayla and then shaking his head to signal to her to disregard what he was saying.

"Good. Just stay where you are. We'll be right down in a few hours to straighten this thing out. You're my friend. Don't worry. I'll take care of everything."

The Duce hung up the phone. "Yeah, I bet you will," he said, under his breath. The Duce tried to rationalize the situation. Why did Chucky have to come to Las Vegas to straighten out the problem? Didn't they just do that over the phone? No, he thought. Chucky would come down with a hit squad and then, *bang! bang!* Two to the back of the head. Then they'd bury him somewhere in the desert. He knew that's the way it would happen because that's what he'd do. Even if there was the slightest chance that someone might rat them out, the mob would whack you. He knew the mob's philosophy: Why take the chance? His mind raced. What would he do to foil their plot? Maybe a preemptive strike on Chucky and the crew. Then he'd sneak back into to Providence and whack anyone who had a hand in the order to execute him, including the Old Man. "Fuck them!" he said to himself, trying to psyche himself up. "I'll kill them all!"

Kayla could see the nervous pensive expression on his face. She stood up and gave him a soft kiss. "What's wrong, Denny?"

Dussault shrugged Kayla off, just murmuring to himself. "I need a piece!"

"A piece. What's that?"

"A gun."

"A gun? Why do you need a gun?"

"Some men are coming here to kill me."

"Who? Why?

"Chucky's coming, and I don't know who else is coming with him."

"Isn't he your best friend? I think you're overacting. This must be just a misunderstanding."

"Make no mistake about it. They'll be here in the evening. They're coming here to kill me...and you."

"Me? Why me?"

"Because you're with me. We pulled a big job and someone fed a bullshit story to the newspapers that said I made a deal with the feds to rat them out. They don't know what I told you."

"Are you sure they're coming here to kill you?"

"Positive. I haven't lived this long in this business without knowing when someone's out to kill me. I'm going to give you some money…enough for you to get away until this either blows over or I'm dead, one way or the other."

Kayla walked into the kitchen and took out a large kitchen knife. "I'm not going anywhere without you. If Chucky comes here to kill us, I'll wait for him in the lobby. I'll put my arms around him and give him a big kiss…like nothing's wrong. Then I'll slice his throat…cut his jugular vein in half," she said, her face flushed with anger.

Dussault knew she was serious. He laughed and swelled up with pride, knowing that his companion, this call girl turned lover, was willing to kill to protect him. He nodded to himself, and in his heart he knew she really cared for him. Then he placed his arms around her and gave her a kiss. "Kayla, you're overacting," he said in jest. "Taking this much too serious," he said, mocking what she had said earlier. "But believe me; I need a piece…something to cut them in half. Where the hell am I going to get hold of a gun?"

Kayla thought for a moment. "I think I can get you a gun. I know the maître d' at the Sands Casino. He also works at the pawn shop where you bought me that necklace. Maybe he can get you a gun. His name is Julian."

"If he works at the Gold Rush Pawn Shop, he most certainly can get me a gun. That place is owned and operated by the Chicago mob."

"How do you know that?

The Duce just raised his eyebrows and nodded as if to tell her something without telling her something.

Kayla picked up the phone, called Julian at the Sands Hotel, and told him briefly the predicament they were in. Then she put the Duce on the phone.

"Julian, I have a beef with some guys back East. I need a piece in case they try to strong-arm Kayla and me."

"Don't worry. I understand. I'll take of it personally. Let say, a half hour."

"Thanks. Kayla wants to talk to you before you hang up."

Kayla talked to Julian, thanking him many times before she hung up.

Dussault paced around the apartment. He was nervous, visibly agitated as the wait seemed to last for over an hour, when in actuality only twenty minutes had passed. He began thinking that Julian wouldn't come through or he was just fluffing him off. Finally there was a knock at the door. A man in his late fifties handed the Duce a long black satchel.

Dussault reached into his pocket and began peeling off a couple of hundred-dollar bills.

"No, no, no," the man said, putting his hands up and refusing to take the money. "Julian said don't worry about it. It's on the house."

"I appreciate that," Dussault said, folding up several hundred-dollar bills. "Take this anyway, and tell Julian he's a lifesaver."

The man took the money and quickly shoved it into his top pocket. "Good hunting," he said, smiling as he made his way down the stairs.

After the man left, Dassault opened the satchel. Much to his surprise and delight, inside the satchel was a pump-action sawed-off shotgun, a half dozen double-O buckshot shells, and several deer slugs. It was more than he expected or needed. It was the ultimate equalizer. For a while he was at ease, relaxed, until he began thinking how many men would come and how they would try to kill him. He and Kayla were hungry, but they didn't want to leave the apartment and be exposed out in the open. He called a local Italian restaurant and ordered a large pizza and some calzones to be delivered.

After they ate, he paced the apartment, occasionally peeking out of the Venetian blinds for any movement in the parking lot. Kayla cleaned the apartment and watered her plants with a large metal watering can, trying to keep busy to take her mind off the uncertainty of what was about to happen. Dussault was tired and began popping amphetamines to stay sharp and alert.

Just before dark, a panel truck drove erratically around the parking lot, stopping and then moving every few seconds. Finally, the van came to a stop in front of their apartment. The Duce opened one of the blinds slightly and recognized that Skippy was driving the van and Chucky was on the passenger side. There appeared to be a third man sitting in the back, but he couldn't make out who it was.

"Here we go," he said to Kayla. "If anything goes wrong, if you hear gunshots, take the bag of money under the bed. Leave by the back exit. Leave Las Vegas, and don't come back unless you hear from me. Got that?"

Kayla nodded nervously.

"Good, because your life will depend on it."

Dussault loaded the shotgun and put the remaining shells into his pants pocket. Then he placed a sports jacket over the gun and opened the door.

"Be careful, Denny," she said kissing and hugging him as he left the apartment.

As Dussault walked down the stairway, he could feel his heart racing, pounding in his chest like a drum roll. If this was to be his last day on earth he would not go down without taking out a few of them, he thought. He knew it could easily come down to kill or be killed, and he was ready for either or both.

As he entered the parking lot, he still hadn't decided his course of action. Should he initiate a preemptive strike, gun blazing? Should he let them make the first move, or listen to what they had to say? As he approached the van, he held his trembling finger on both triggers of the shotgun.

Chucky opened the door to the van and smiled a becoming smile. The Duce looked in the backseat of the van and saw that it was JoJo Dancer. When Chuckey saw the shotgun under Dussault's jacket, he froze, his smile disappeared, and his expression turned into one of fear.

"What the fuck is this?" he asked nervously. "I told you I'm your friend. We just came here to straighten everything out."

"Everyone relax," the Duce said, taking his jacket off the shotgun. "You think I'm fuckin' stupid! I'm the Duce, not the dunce! Chucky, Chucky, Chucky. You're my best friend, and here's my other good friends." He looked at Skippy and JoJo. You needed three guys just to talk? Did you already dig the hole in the desert, or were you going to do that afterward?"

"Swear to God," Chucky said, holding up his right hand. "We're just here to talk."

"Okay, you want to talk? Then we'll talk. You come with me upstairs, Chucky. My other two friends stay in the van," he said.

From his years of playing poker, he knew that at the moment he was holding the strongest hand and when to pull a bluff that would not be called. "Oh, by the way, Skippy and JoJo, since Chucky left Vegas, I put together my own crew. They're watching us right now," he said, looking up at the second-floor windows, "with rifles. So if I were you, I wouldn't get out of the van to have a cigarette or take a piss. Relax and stay put."

"Whatever you say, Duce," Skippy said.

After Chucky entered the apartment, Dussault closed the door and slid across the dead bolt.

Chucky saw Kayla and smiled a nervous, forced smile. He slowly reached into his top pocket and removed the newspaper article and handed it to Dussault.

"This is why we're here, Denny," he said, not knowing if the Duce had told Kayla his real name.

"Sit down here," Dussault said, pointing to the kitchen table with his shotgun.

Dussault read the article, expressing no sign of emotion. Finally, he grinned. "Can't you see this is all bullshit? I ain't never talked with the FBI or that Jew lawyer, what was his name,

Goldstein? Couldn't the wops in Providence see the story was a plant? You reacted exactly the way they wanted you to. For all I know, the law followed you here. I've done time rather than rat, and you of all people know that, Chucky. So that dumb Patriarca panicked. He called Mister C. Mister C. called the Frenchman, and he called you to come out and whack me. Is that about right?"

Kayla picked up the article and began reading it in silence and amazement, with a frozen expression on her face. She read the details of what was described as one of the most bizarre and largest heists in Rhode Island's history. She also came to learn that the man she knew as Dennis Allen was in reality Robert "The Duce" Dussault, the lead gunman in the infamous Bonded Vault robbery.

"Fuck the Providence mob," Dussault said. "For all you know, they're conspiring with the Frenchman to get us to whack each other and split up the rest of the loot from the heist. Let's leave it all behind, Chucky. Start a new life. Pool our money and buy a strip mall or an apartment complex and live off the income. You and your fiancée, Kayla and me. We'll live like kings and queens. We'll never have to look over our shoulders again. Maybe every now and then we'll pull down a score," he said, joking, trying to convince Chucky to go along with his plan. "Why this doesn't make sense?"

Kayla's eyes lit up. "Come on, Chucky. This sounds great. Talk with your fiancée. She'll tell you this is the right thing to do."

"For the time being," the Duce said, "how are you going to square this with the Providence mob?"

"I'll do it right now. Kayla, give me the phone." Chucky dialed a long-distance number. The Frenchman picked up the phone. "Remy, it's me, Chucky."

"Did you deliver the package?"

"No. I'm here with the Duce. He told me he never talked with the feds or that lawyer, and I believe him. He said the story was a plant to flush him out. You know the Duce. He'd never rat us out. Remember that robbery in Lowell when the Duce got pinched and did a nickel rather than rat on Lucky and his crew? That's the kind of guy he is. He knows it'll be a death sentence ratting out the Old Man. You tell the Old man he's a stand-up guy. As far as I'm concerned, it's over. It was a wasted trip."

"Then come back. If you say he's okay, then I guess he's okay. I'll try to square it with the Old Man. I won't say you can bet your life that it'll be squashed, because if anything goes south, you already have. Catch my drift?"

Chucky hung up the phone and told the Duce what the Frenchman said, all but the last part.

"You know my life is in your hands if anything goes wrong," Chucky said.

"As mine was in yours an hour ago," Dussault quickly replied.

Dussault put the gun under the table, stood up, and hugged Chucky. "When I go back to Providence, I'll tell my fiancée what you propose. If she agrees, and I'm sure she will, we'll be back after we get married. And maybe we can leave this life behind us and become legitimate businessmen."

"Work on convincing Remy that the Old Man has nothing to worry about. You know how those Guineas in Providence are calabrese."

"Don't worry. I'll take care of it."

After Chuckey left, Dussault watched the van until it was out of sight. He wondered if the phone conversation with the Frenchman was a ruse to put him at ease and they would return to whack him.

He also wondered when Chucky returned to Providence without carrying out the Old Man's orders if he would get whacked. If that happened, Patriarca would send another hit squad, men he would not recognize, and he'd be marked for death once again.

Bonnie and Clyde

Christmas, 1974

Dussault thought it was unwise to stay in Las Vegas in the event that Chucky's hit squad or another group of assassins would be or ordered to whack him and Kayla. He decided to take a trip until he was sure the contract the Old Man had put out on his life was canceled. He was not naïve to the way the mafia operated. He was growing exceedingly paranoid because he knew that once an execution order had been given, it was seldom rescinded. His anxiety became accelerated by the fact that he had tried to call Chucky at his home and his fiancée's apartment and could not reach them. Maybe, he thought, they had been whacked because Chucky did not carry out the Old Man's orders. Maybe another hit squad was now looking for him.

Before they left, Dussault went to see Paulie at the MGM to get some more drugs. He got two small plastic bags containing black beauties, which were even more powerful amphetamines that obies, and another bag of Librium to help him come down so he could fall asleep at night.

Kayla was driving to the Hyatt Regency Hotel several hundred miles from Las Vegas. As it became nighttime, Dussault popped a few Librium and fell into a deep sleep. Now that Kayla knew the full extent of the Duce's criminal activities, she was having second thoughts about her current and future relationship with him. She had some serious soul searching to do and endless miles to think about her decision. Since the confrontation with Chucky, Dussault had become exceedingly paranoid, morphing into someone unrecognizable and becoming a dangerous, unpredictable man.

It was 1:00 a.m., and there were no other cars on the long stretch of dark highway. Her mind digressed. She remembered seeing the Warren Beatty, Faye Dunnaway movie, *Bonnie and Clyde*. She could recall vividly the ending of the movie when the pair of criminal lovers were riddled in a hail of gunfire at a law enforcement ambush. Was this to be her and the Duce's fate? Would the mob find them and execute them first? What would her mother, brother, and friends think of her life ending that way? Would she be arrested with Dussault as his accomplice and spend decades in prison? He was becoming self-destructive, and the drugs were only accelerating his downward spiral. He was now capable of anything, and maybe, she thought, even killing her. As she looked over at Dussault sleeping, she knew there was another way out, but she was not ready to make that decision.

When Dussault awoke, he was jumpy, constantly checking the rearview mirror. Every time a car passed them or was driving too close behind them, he thought they were being followed. It was late morning when they checked into the Hyatt Regency Hotel. They slept until the next morning.

Before they went out for breakfast, the Duce told her he was going to the liquor store to pick up a bottle of Jack Daniels Whiskey. He took a small bag from the dresser draw and popped a few black beauties into his mouth.

"Don't you think you've had enough of those?" Kayla said. "You're turning into a junkie!"

Dussault turned around, enraged. "A junkie!" He slapped her across her face, that was more like a punch. "You better smarten the fuck up!" he said, slamming the door behind him.

Kayla finally realized the honeymoon was over. How quickly their relationship had disintegrated. As she looked at her reddened, swollen face in the hotel mirror, she knew she had to leave. She quickly packed her suitcase. Suddenly, a thought entered her mind. In his state of mind, what would he do if he came back before she could make a clean getaway? She halfheartedly made a phone call to ensure her safety.

When Dussault returned to the hotel, the door to his room was open. He entered cautiously, not knowing why it was open. He saw Kayla and two well-dressed men standing beside her. Immediately, he knew they were detectives.

"What's going on here?" he asked defiantly.

"Mr. Allen, your wife called. There is clear evidence of domestic abuse. She doesn't want to press charges. All she wants to do is leave without another altercation, and we're here to see that she leaves safely."

"At least she didn't rat me out," the Duce thought. "No problem. We just had a little marital argument."

"It appears by her bruises that it was a little more than a *little* argument."

Kayla left without looking at Dussault or saying a word. The two detectives escorted her to the parking lot, and she left with them.

Dussault sat in the room the rest of the day, polishing off the bottle of Jack Daniels. He was depressed. He knew he had fucked up. The best woman he ever had in his life was gone. Maybe, he thought, she would return to her apartment in Las Vegas, and he would make up with her. He would apologize and buy her something expensive and make amends. He was confident he could make it right. The next morning, he drove back to Las Vegas.

New Year's Day, 1975

Dussault had been back in Las Vegas for two days. The apartment manager let him in with his pass key and made a duplicate key for him. He waited for her at the apartment, expecting her to pop in any moment. He took off the air-conditioner grill and hid the shotgun ammunition and a valise of money behind the ductwork. He looked through Kayla's rolodex and called her mother and brother. He told them he was her boyfriend and just had returned from a business trip and was looking for her. He told them that he was staying at her apartment and that if she called, to have her call him.

Little did Dussault know that Kayla had stayed at a hotel and then flew to her mother's house in San Diego, California. When her brother told her that her boyfriend, Dennis, had called and was staying at her apartment, she became livid.

Kayla called the apartment complex manager and told him to put him out. "If you let him in without my permission, then you do whatever is necessary to get him out," she said, screaming at him. "Make sure he's out before I get back next week!"

That evening, Dussault was watching the nightly news when there was a knock at the door. He was lying on the bed in his bathrobe, sipping a bottle of beer. He jumped up quickly, and a wide smile appeared on his face. He thought that Kayla had finally returned. When he opened the door, several Las Vegas policemen in uniform and several plainclothes detectives burst into the room with their guns drawn. They pushed him to the floor, put his hands behind his back, and handcuffed him.

"That miserable bastard ratted me out," he thought. "What's going on here?" he shouted.

The police didn't answer him. They let him dress and read him his Miranda Rights. As they shoved him into the back of a patrol car, the occupants of the apartment complex came out to see what was causing all the commotion.

The Las Vegas police took Dussault's fingerprints and ran the license and social security card he gave them under the name of Dennis Allen from Great Neck, New York. They ran the information through the

BCI computer network, and it came up clean. Then they placed him in the interrogation room. The Duce believed he could con his way of this mess. It all depended upon what Kayla had told the apartment complex manager and the police.

Dussault kept asking them for his phone call. He figured that a sharp lawyer would have him out in a few hours, and then he'd disappear. The detectives kept asking him questions like, "Where is the money? Who are your accomplices?" Dussault kept adamantly responding that he didn't know what they were talking about.

An hour later a well-dressed man with a marine-style haircut entered the interrogation room. He studied Dussault's features carefully, without saying a word. "Good day, Mr. Allen. I'm Agent Ronald Wright with the FBI."

"Well, it's about time," Dussault said, leaning forward. "I don't know why I'm here, and the LVPD won't tell me."

Agent Wright didn't answer him. He turned to the detective who was standing behind Dussault. "Didn't I tell your chief to look at the surveillance tape from the robbery? He's not one of the robbers."

"How can you be so sure?"

"Because," Agent Wright said, in a tone expressing his displeasure, "all the bank robbers were clean shaven. This man could not have grown a full beard in two days, that's how!

Let him go."

The Duce breathe a sigh of relief. They had nothing on him. Kayla had not told them who he really was. "You know, Agent Wright, they didn't even let me make a phone call. I'm going to have to call someone to pick me up."

"I'll let you make your phone call now," the detective behind Dussault said, "but first

you have to sign a few papers."

"I ain't signing nothing," Dussault said defiantly. He thought they were trying to trick him. "You have no PC to hold me."

Dussault had been a few minutes away from getting released, but he had overplayed his hand. Agent Wright became more than curious about his choice of words. When Dussault said PC, Agent Wright knew it meant "probable cause," which was not a common term used by ordinary citizens. Then Wright looked at the tattoo Dussault had on his bicep, which was in dark indigo ink: "Duce."

"Don't worry, Mr. Allen," Wright said. "I'll be back in five minutes to speed up your release."

Agent Wright left the interrogation room and ran the nickname Duce through the BCI database and the tattoo through the bureau of prisons database. Five minutes later he returned to the interrogation room holding several papers in his hand. "Mr. Allen, your name is Dennis Allen, is it not?"

"Sure is," the Duce said calmly but with conviction and confidence.

Agent Wright placed one of the papers he was holding in front of Dussault. It was a mug shot of Dussault from Danbury Prison. The other paper contained a warrant for his arrest in connection with the Bonded Vault robbery. "You can make your phone call now, Duce," Wright said, with a cat-that-ate-the-canary grin on his face, "but you're not going anywhere for a long, long time, Mr. Robert 'The Duce' Dussault."

Killing Two Birds with One Stone

January 2, 1975

All law enforcement authorities in Rhode Island were informed that Dussault had been apprehended. Immediately, Verde placed all known associates of Dussault under twenty-four-hour surveillance, fearing that when the details of the Duce's arrest hit the newspapers, they would all disappear.

Detective Stone entered Verde's office at 8:00 a.m. She was radiant, and Verde could not hide the wide schoolboy grin on his face, which did not escape her notice. "Good morning, Rose. Would you like a coffee or a muffin?"

"No, thank you. I ate breakfast before I went to the gym for my morning workout."

"We have some work to do before we leave. Colonel Stone has already dispatched Detective Mancuso from your office to start the preliminary interrogation of Dussault. We're flying to Las Vegas tomorrow at seven a.m."

"Together?"

Verde smiled. "You can take along your mother as a chaperone, if you like," he said in jest.

Stone was perturbed by his condescending quip and quickly changed the subject. "Do you have a strategy in mind to get him to confess?"

"Not yet. He's a hardened criminal, a tough nut to crack. Even though he's not Italian, he abides by their code: omerta."

"Omerta?"

"Code of silence. Cooperation or talking to anyone in law enforcement is a violation punishable by death."

"Then how are we going to get him to testify against his accomplices in the robbery?"

"We're going to have to be creative. Use every trick in the book and maybe some deceptive coercion that isn't in the book," he said, raising his eyebrows. "We'll have to put the cliché to the test that you can't con a conman. Are you sure I can't get you something?"

"I'm fine."

"Well then, maybe you can do something for me?"

"And that is…?"

"Smile once in a while, Rose. Just smile."

She shook her head, rolled her eyes, and gave him a false smile, which insinuated to him to fuck off.

"Then I guess I'll see you at the airport tomorrow morning."

*

The next morning, they flew from Green Airport in Rhode Island to Logan Airport in Boston before boarding a nonstop flight to Las Vegas. Verde and Stone were studying the Dussault file. Verde had formulated a profile of him, looking for anything that could be used as leverage to coerce the Duce into cooperating with the investigation.

Midway in their journey, Verde looked over at Stone and began daydreaming. He envisioned her sitting naked beside him. He was so entranced, savoring the vision, that he didn't realize that she was staring at the blank, satiated expression on his face.

"What could he be thinking about?" she thought. "What could possibly have brought that lustful look in his eyes?" Finally, she interrupted his blissful stare. "What? What are you daydreaming about?"

Her voice brought him back to reality. "Oh, nothing," he said, looking back down at the Dussault file.

Stone went back to studying her file. She placed it on her lap, leaned over, and closed Verde's file. "I'd like to know what you were thinking about. I have an idea, but I'd like to hear it from you."

Verde smiled and then reopened the file. Stone closed it again. "Are you going to tell me?"

"You *really* want to know? How would you know if I was telling you the truth?"

"I have a pretty good idea. I'm not naïve. I've seen that look before. Tell me."

"All right. All I will tell you is what I remember from the social psychology class I took."

"And that is?"

Verde smiled. "This is foreplay," he thought. He could never tell her what he was really thinking. It would only serve to put more distance between them. She would despise him even more, he thought. He decided to tell her something close to the truth. If she became outraged, he would tell her he was lying, studying her response, playing her, and trying to rattle her in preparation for the Dussault interrogation.

"Well, I remember when it came to the subject of social interaction and attraction with the opposite sex."

"And?" she said, leaning forward in her chair.

"When a male and female are in close proximity, as we are, they both measure the potential of a sexual encounter between them."

Stone squinted her eyes, trying to grasp what he had just said. "And that's what you were doing, imagining having sex with me?"

"Not exactly. I was interrupted before I got to that. You might say," he said with a grin, "it was coitus interruptus."

Stone gave him an odd look and shook her head as if to say no way. "If that's what you were really daydreaming about...dream on." Stone was going to resume reading the file, but she put it aside. "Was that what you were really thinking, or am I being played? Is this another test?"

"You'll never know, but it wouldn't be out of the realm of behavior for a normal, heterosexual male to have such fantasies, especially when sitting next to a beautiful and sexy woman in close proximity."

Verde opened the Dussault file and resumed reading. Out of the corner of his eye, he noticed that Rose had slight but detectable smile, which she quickly suppressed, and he was pleased.

■■

Upon arrival in Las Vegas, they checked into the Stardust Hotel in separate adjacent rooms. Just before Stone entered her room, she turned to Verde. "Isn't this one of the casinos that was on the undesirable list because it's owned and operated by organized crime?"

Verde smiled. "They all are. The owners of record are straw men who operate the casinos and hotels for the mob. Get some rest, and we'll see if we can crack Dussault this afternoon."

Later in the day, Detectives Stone and Mancuso and two detectives from the LVPD were in the interrogation viewing room, observing Dussault through one-way mirrored glass. As Verde entered the interrogation room, the audio and video recording devices were turned on.

Dussault was sitting behind a long green metal table, slouched over in his chair. His hair and clothing were disheveled. The room was stark. The walls were painted faded green. The only objects in the room was the metal table, two folding chairs, an old yellowed clock, and recording cameras placed high up on the walls.

"Good afternoon, Mr. Dussault," Verde said, in a straightforward, businesslike manner. "I'm FBI Agent Vincent Verde, with the Rhode Island office of the FBI."

Dussault straightened up in his chair. "Wow, if it's not the legendary Jay Verde," he said, as if he were greeting an old friend.

"You know me."

"Better than you think," the Duce said in a confident, cocky manner. "I served time with your brother in Walpole. I can see the family resemblance. You know he idolized you. He talked about you all the time."

"And that interested you."

"Never know when a stray piece of information about the opposition might come in handy. Maybe keep me one step ahead of the law and out of prison."

"And how has that been working out for you so far?" Verde asked, taunting him.

Detectives Stone, Mancuso, and the LVPD detectives were listening attentively "What's he doing in there?" Stone asked.

"Oh, he's smart," Mancuso said. "Verde's putting him at ease. You know, chitchat, small talk, nothing confrontational. They're feeling each other out."

"In Walpole I played on the prison baseball team. Not that I was any good," he said, lighting up a cigarette. "Being outside in the sun instead of the bullshit details in the laundry or picking up trash or working in the mess hall for a dollar a day—fuck that! We won the New England prison championship. Largely due to your brother. After the season ended, the warden scheduled a special game with the Cape Cod All-Stars. They were going to play a series of games in the East Coast All-Star games to showcase their talent before big-league scouts. Their coach wanted a tune up game before they left to play because he heard that we had a pitcher with pro stuff, your brother.

"Believe it or not, going into the seventh inning, we were up one to zilch because your brother was pitching a no-hitter. Then he ran out of gas, and our relief pitcher gave up six runs. After the game, their coach comes over to our dugout to talk with our coach and your brother. I overheard only bits and pieces of his conversation. He says something to the effect that it's a shame that your brother took the wrong path in life because he could have easily made it to the big time. And because of his age, and his criminal record, the window of opportunity had passed him by."

Stone was growing impatient. "Why isn't he starting the interrogation?"

"Actually he is," Detective Mancuso said. "Once he has established a rapport, he'll go to work."

"Actually," Verde said. flipping through Dussault's file, "the window of opportunity has passed both my brother and you by. Very soon, all you'll have left is your past and no future. Maybe I can change that."

"Maybe the window of opportunity has also passed you by, Verde," the Duce said, trying to turn the tables on him.

"How do you figure that?"

"Yes, I've led a criminal life. I don't apologize for one day of it. I have no regrets. Can you say the same, Verde? My philosophy has always been it's better to live a short life as a king than a long life as a peasant. Only recently did I believe that I could have had a normal life. Leave the life of crime behind. Get married and have a couple of kids. But it wasn't to be. I fucked up. But I look at you. A big-shot job. A big-shot title. Nice high-paying career. You're a good-looking guy. Nothin' homo intended," he said as they both laughed. "But I don't see a ring on your finger. Where's the wife? Where's the kids? Where's the home in the suburbs with the white picket fence? All you got is your job."

Stone observed the expression on Verde's face and reflected on what Dussault said. "How cunning this Dussault is," she thought. "He's profiling Verde." She realized that everything he just said to Verde also applied to her life. For the first time, she felt like a kindred spirit with him.

"The difference is, this is the life and future I've chosen for myself. From this day forward, your life and future is the one the criminal justice system and I will choose for you. Maybe if you cooperate, you may have a say in your destiny, maybe not. You can never compare the decisions you've made in your life to mine."

"Really? How are you ever going to have a stable life and relationship if you're chasing around guys like me twenty-four seven? What's the divorce rate among cops? I bet it's even higher with those in the bureau. When everything is said and done, we're both going to end up the same—alone and lonely. We'll both be buried somewhere with no one to mourn our passing except maybe a few kin. Yessiree, that's our destiny, no legacy at all. No one to carry on our names, and after a while, no one will even remember we ever existed."

"Maybe you're right. And if you are, I can live with that. If my brother told you anything meaningful about me, you know right well I could have easily have chosen the path he did. I would have been a made guy by now. But this is the life I've chosen, and I have no regrets in my decision."

"So do I, Verde. So do I."

"Well, I guess it's time to get down to business. We have two witnesses who positively identified you as the lead gunman in the Bonded Vault Heist," he said, pushing three papers stapled together in front of him.

"What's this?"

"It's the plea agreement you asked your lawyer to get for you. He got everything you asked for. It's signed by the Rhode Island Attorney General and me."

Dussault pushed the folder back toward Verde. "That agreement is bullshit! I never talked with Goldstein or the FBI. I'm not a rat. I'll never rat. There's nothing you can do or say that will make me inform on my friends. I'd rather do 'all day' than cooperate with the law. I wouldn't put it past you if you fed that false story to the newspapers. Oh yes, I think it was you! Shove that plea agreement up your ass. That story almost got me killed!"

In the surveillance room, Stone nodded her head. "He's smarter than he looks," she said to Mancuso.

"After that article hit the newspapers," Mancuso said, "we're lucky we got to him before the mob did. If Patriarca did sanction the heist, he's going to have everyone who could link him to the robbery executed."

Suddenly, Stone remembered what Verde said in his office that it was an acceptable practice to deceive a criminal in order to trap him. Her eyes glazed over as she quickly formulated a false narrative in her mind. "You're right. Patriarca will most certainly have everyone killed that could send him back to prison." Then she turned to the two LVPD detectives. "Do you have any photographs of violent murders that took place here? Shotgun blasts to the face or bodies bludgeoned to make them unrecognizable?"

"Maybe," one of the detectives replied. "Why do you have in mind?"

"Get me as many as possible. Also get me the BCI photographs of two of Dussault's closest friends and associates, Chuckey Floyd and Skippy Burns."

After the detectives left, she told Mancuso her plan. "Call Verde on the intercom and have him come in here," she said, with growing excitement.

Verde did not know why he was called out of the interrogation room. When he entered the surveillance room Stone had removed her jacket and was placing her holster and ankle gun on a table. Then she unbuttoned the first two buttons on her blouse and adjusted her bra exposing her cleavage

"What's this?" Verde asked, with a puzzled smile on his face.

"Listen to the plan Stone came up with," Mancuso said. "You'll love it."

Verde listened to her plan. They rehearsed a few finer points. When the LVPD detective came back into the room, Stone flipped through the gruesome photographs to find the most suitable ones. Then she placed the mug shots of Floyd and Burns on top of the photographs and placed them in a file.

Dussault smiled as she entered the room. "Which one are you, the good cop or the bad cop?" he asked, checking out her figure.

"Neither. I'm a secretary."

As Stone went to place the file in front of where Verde would be sitting, she purposely tripped, sending the photographs scattering across the table. As she leaned over, she noticed that the Duce was looking down her blouse and then at what she was collecting. She slowly placed the photographs back in the file, placing some of the gruesome pictures and the mug shots of Floyd and Burns on top to make sure Dussault had seen them.

"I'm sorry what happened to your friends," she said apologetically.

"Sorry about what?" he asked, checking out her cleavage once again.

"Oh, I may have misspoken. I guess they didn't tell you yet. Please don't get me in trouble and tell that FBI agent I said anything."

"Don't worry about anything, sweetheart. I'll keep it between you and me," he said, winking. "But what is it I'm supposed to know?"

"I think I already told you too much. I'm sure that FBI guy will tell you if you ask him."

After she went back into the surveillance room, they all observed Dussault looking around the room. Verde waited until Dussault flipped up the first few pages of the file before he entered. As Verde entered the room, the Duce quickly closed the file and sat back nonchalantly in his chair.

Verde sat down, opened the file, and flipped through the photographs slowly. Then he stared at Dussault and smiled.

"What is it that you're not telling me, Verde? What, you arrested Skippy and Chucky?" he asked in a cocky tone, as if he had been privy to confidential information. "If you did, you arrested the wrong guys."

"Jesus Christ," Verde said, feigning anger. "This just came over the teletype. How could you have known? That secretary. That stupid secretary. I'll have her job!"

"Relax. It's nothing I hadn't already suspected."

"We didn't arrest Chuckey. It's not that we didn't want to. You said earlier that when the article about you was in the newspaper, you almost got whacked. Let me tell you what I think happened. You can stop me if you think I'm wrong. The article comes out. The Old Man panics. He puts a contract out on you. Chucky and a few others involved in the robbery are ordered to whack you. Friends killing friends. Yeah, you know that's how the mob works. The crew comes to Vegas, and for some reason they come back without carrying out Patriarca's orders. Sound about right?"

Dussault didn't answer him. He just sat back in his chair, listening attentively to what Verde was saying.

"Now let me tell you how you see your current situation. You won't rat. After all you're a...*stand-up guy*," Verde said, mocking him. You figure you get eight years for Bonded Vault and serve maybe five. You think you'll have, what, a half million waiting for you when you get out. Well, that's never going to happen! At least the second part. As I see it, you were supposed to be the first one whacked. Then the Frenchman sold you and all the rest of your accomplices out to protect the Old Man. Then he took the rest of the Bonded Vault loot and split it with the Old Man."

"Nice story, Verde, but you know that's all bullshit."

"Is it now? We know you've been to Chucky's house on Golf Street in East Providence. Your fingerprints are all over the place, and so is your pals Chucky and Skippy's brains. Yeah, you heard me right! They got whacked, gangland style, two days ago. Did they kill them for not whacking you, or is the Old Man trying to eliminate everyone who can link him to the robbery?"

Dussault's jaw dropped. He tried to compose himself. He did not want Verde to see that he was rattled. At first he thought he was being played, another false narrative, like the planted story. Still, everything Verde was saying was plausible and highly likely, but he still wasn't convinced.

"And do you want to hear the best part?" Verde said, with a sense of excitement to dramatize and accentuate what he was about to say next, which he felt was his coup de grace, that one final piece of information to convince Dussault that his friends were really executed.

"An arrest warrant for JoJo Dancer was issued for their murder. Not only were his fingerprints on the spent shotgun shells, but the next-door neighbor identified him as entering and leaving the house the day of their murders."

That was it. Dussault was convinced Verde was telling him the truth. He knew that was probably exactly how it went down. In a twisted way, he was saddened by the fact that Chucky and Skippy were killed for not carrying out Patriarca's orders. And he also knew that's the way the mob operated. He also figured that JoJo was probably executed that very same day. More often than not, the killer ends up being killed to cut off the information trail leading to the person who gave the original order.

"So here's what I propose," Verde said placing the plea agreement and a pen in front of him. "You sign the agreement and testify for the DA.

We'll give you immunity from prosecution, a new identity, a job, and a home where the mob will never find you. We'll put you in protective custody until the trial is over."

"Sounds like a good deal, Verde, but I can't sign it. I'll do the time."

"If you won't cooperate, then you're of no use to me. Let's face it; you're a drowning man. I can either throw you a life preserver or an anchor. Cut the deal or else!"

"Or else what?" Dussault asked defiantly.

"I'll see to it personally that when you are returned to Rhode Island, I have you put into the ACI's general population. How long do you think you're going to stay alive there…a week, maybe? Why the LVPD have already started a pool on how long you last in prison."

"I said no deal. Don't worry about me. I can take care of myself."

"I know you're a smart guy. Think of your future because from where I'm standing, you don't have one. There's no more money from the heist. The Old Man killed all your friends. Isn't it time for a little payback?"

"I know that everything you're saying is the right thing to do. But that's just not me. That's not the Duce. I want my phone call and my lawyer."

"I'll be leaving Vegas tomorrow morning. You'll be transferred back to Rhode Island tomorrow afternoon. If you don't sign the deal before I leave, the deal is off the table." Verde up to leave. "And by the way," he added, just before closing the door behind him without looking back, "pleasant dreams."

When Verde entered the surveillance room, Stone smiled. "Perfect, but he didn't sign the plea agreement."

"Give him time to think about what will happen to him if he doesn't cooperate. Don't worry; he'll sign. It was a brilliant ruse."

"Actually, it was Mancuso who gave me the idea for the false narrative."

***

When they arrived at the Stardust Hotel, there was a message at the front desk for them from the LVPD that stated Dussault had signed the agreement and that his confession and the details of the robbery would be taped tomorrow at 10:00 a.m.

Verde and Stone went to their rooms. Just before he entered, Verde turned to her and said, "We just killed two birds with one stone," he said, as they both smiled at his pun.

"How do you figure that?"

"First, your plan was so clever that the Duce was absolutely convinced that Chucky and Skippy had been whacked. Secondly, what alternative did your false narrative leave him but to sign the agreement? In all the years I've been in law enforcement, this was one of the most crafty and devious plans," he said, raising his eyebrows, "I've ever been involved in. As it was unfolding, it was exhilarating. It was almost better than...than...having sex."

"Really?"

"Well, I said almost," he said as they both laughed. "Later, if you like, we can go out to dinner to celebrate."

"I'd like that."

When Stone entered her room, a sense of euphoria enveloped her from her achievement and Verde's praise. She now felt that he had finally accepted her as his equal.

Who's on Top

Verde made reservations at the Galaxy Restaurant located on the second floor next to the high rollers' gambling room at the Stardust Hotel. He dressed in a dark-blue pinstriped suit and an open-collar light-blue shirt. He knocked on Stone's door and was pleasantly surprised to see that instead of wearing her mundane dark-green business suit, she wore a light-beige cocktail dress and sheer nylon stockings with matching pumps. She wore her hair up and put on a little more makeup than usual. She put on a floral perfume, and Verde drank in the captivating fragrance.

"You look beautiful," he said, holding her hand and giving her a slight spin as he examined her from head to foot. "And you even wore a dress for our first date," he said, in jest.

Stone rolled her eyes. "Can't you ever give it a rest?" She grabbed her purse as she closed the door behind her.

"Not when I'm going to accompany the most beautiful woman in Las Vegas."

Stone felt awkward and did not respond to his compliment. She didn't want to encourage his advances.

When they entered the restaurant, there was a long line of people waiting to enter. Verde gave the maître d' his name, and they were escorted to their table.

The restaurant was spacious and decorated with live palm trees, sequoia cactus, and assorted citrus and floral trees. Behind their table was a rock waterfall with the sound of cascading water trickling into a pond below. The large pond was filled with aquatic plants and large, brightly colored Koi fish swimming slowly about. The tall ceilings were painted black with blinking recessed lights that resembled stars. Occasionally a programmed lighting system would display what appeared to be an aurora borealis and shooting stars that streaked across the faux sky.

The waiter took their order. Stone ordered a Caesar salad, which was prepared at their table. They both ordered filet mignon, medium-well. A short while later, the maître d' came to their table with a monogrammed tablecloth slung over his arm and two tall wine glasses in his right hand. Following behind him was a waiter wheeling a tray with a chilled bottle of Dom Perignon in an ice bucket.

"Good evening, Mr. Verde and Miss Stone," the maître d' said. "Welcome to the Galaxy. Mister Rosenthal would like you to enjoy your dinner with a complementary bottle of champagne."

Verde looked up surprised. "Thank you, but that really won't be necessary."

"Mr. Rosenthal insists."

"In that case, tell him thank you from the both of us."

The maître d' unfastened the metal binding of the bottle, placed the tablecloth on top, and twisted it gently, easing out the cork until it popped. Then he filled their wine glasses.

"Enjoy," he said. "If there's anything else I can get you, ask your waiter to inform me."

After the maître d' left, Stone took a sip. "Don't you think that was odd? Who is this Rosenthal?"

Verde took a sip and nodded, signifying that it was excellent. "The owner of record is Allen Glick. He's a squeaky-clean front man, but Rosenthal operates this casino for the mob. They keep a black book of undesirables to keep out criminals. They also keep a green book for dignitaries, county commissioners, the gaming commission, and especially those in law enforcement. They knew who we were the minute I made our reservation."

As they were eating, Stone noticed that Verde was once again staring at her in a trance.

"What is it, Verde? What are you daydreaming about now?"

Verde snapped out of it. "Do you mind if I ask you a personal question?"

She took another sip of the champagne and shrugged her shoulders. "It all depends on the question."

"You're a beautiful woman. Do you ever think about getting married, settling down, maybe have a couple of children?" he asked, in a serious tone.

Stone choked on the champagne and cleared her throat. The question had caught her off guard. Then she remembered what Dussault had said to Verde in the interrogation room about men like them ending up without a wife and family and dying alone and lonely with no one to morn their passing.

"No, not really," she said, then paused. "Well, to be honest, sometimes. But I have my career. And if this is a marriage proposal," she said, trying to bring a little levity to the serious question he asked, "the answer is no."

They both laughed, but as she ate her dinner, she became solemn. She could feel that maybe he was more than infatuated with her, that maybe he was developing serious feelings and intentions for her.

After they were done eating, Verde asked the waiter for the check. Once again, the maître d' came over and asked them if they enjoyed the meal.

"It was perfect," Verde said.

"And how was your meal, Miss Stone?"

"Equally perfect."

The maître d' told them that their meal was compliments of Mr. Rosenthal. Then he reached into his top pocket. "If it fits into your schedule, I have complimentary tickets to the late-night performance of Wayne Newton here at our Stardust Ballroom. He puts on a fabulous show."

"You've been much too kind," Verde said. "Be sure to thank Mr. Rosenthal for us."

"I will. He believes that we must honor our guests, especially those in law enforcement. Enjoy the rest of your evening."

On his way out, Verde discretely slipped the maître d' and the waiter each a fifty-dollar bill.

They had some time before the show started, so they walked around the casino, watching the gamblers playing roulette, craps, and blackjack. The casino was filled with cigarette smoke and the clanking and ringing of bells from the slot machines.

A scantily clad waitress came up to them. "Would you or your wife like a drink?" she asked.

"I'm all set, but my wife," he said, in a joking manner, "might like something. Honey, would you like a drink?"

"No, thank you, *honey*," she said, mocking what he had said with a wide, disingenuous smile.

"Rose, you should smile more often. You're radiant when you smile, even when it's a sarcastic smile."

In response she curtsied and gave him another sarcastic smile.

Just before the show began, they were escorted to an exclusive section of the theater and seated in an alcove in the front row. Occasionally, a waitress would come to their seats and give them complimentary drinks. There were two preliminary acts. The first was an up-and-coming female comedian named Joan Rivers followed by a Russian juggling troop. When Wayne Newton took the stage, he received a standing ovation. He was accompanied by a full orchestra and several backup singers. He sang many of his standards and finished by singing his signature songs "Danke Schoen," "Daddy Don't You Walk So Fast," and "Red Roses for a Blue Lady."

After the show, they took the elevator to their rooms. They were both mildly drunk. As the elevator came to an abrupt stop, Verde held on to Stone's arm to keep her from stumbling backward.

Stone opened her door.

"Good night, Rose," Verde said. "I had a wonderful night."

"I did too. Come in for a while."

As Verde entered the room, Rose plopped herself on the edge of the bed, kicked off her shoes, and began taking off her nylon stockings. Verde sat down on a chair next to the bed. He was puzzled and wondered if in her intoxicated state if she realized that she was undressing in front of him.

"I really think that I should be going. We have a big day tomorrow," he said, getting up to leave.

"Before you go," she said, standing up, "perhaps you could help me with the clasp in the back of my dress?" She turned her back to him.

"All righty, it's done, and I must be going. Rose, I don't know where this is going, but I think you've had too much to drink. I don't want to take advantage of you."

"Maybe we've both had too much to drink," she said, slipping out of her dress. "Did you ever think that maybe I'm taking advantage of you? I know you've been stripping me naked in your mind ever since we met. Come on, big boy; don't you want to see what you've been dreaming about?"

With those words, she removed his jacket, unfastened the belt on his pants, and unzipped his pants. Then using her leg, she pushed down his pants until they were down to his ankles. She unbuttoned his shirt slowly, pulled off his T-shirt, and flung them across the room. Then she pulled down his blue boxer shorts. She turned around. "Unsnap my bra," she said, almost like a command rather than a request. When her bra was off, she slipped out of her panties one leg at a time, stumbling as she picked up each leg.

They were both naked. Verde became fully erect as he admired her sleek, toned body and the taut, lean mussels in her midsection and abdomen. Her breasts were medium sized and perfectly proportioned for her body. In her heightened state of arousal, her nipples were hard and protruding. She put both her arms around him and began kissing him passionately as he caressed her backside with both hands.

Rose took his hand, led him across the room, tore back the sheets, and gave him a shove, sending him backward on the bed. As she then climbed on top of him, Verde smiled at her aggression. "Knowing your dominant personality," Verde said, toying with her, "I knew you'd want to be on top."

"Knowing your dominant personality, I knew you'd want to be on top," she replied, toying with him. "That's why I took the initiative. I beat you to the punch."

"Maybe I prefer it when the woman is on top."

She straddled him, reached down, and pushed his manhood deeply into her. Verde knew she was in a high state of arousal as he entered her because she was already dripping wet.

Rose arched her back and began gyrating slowly and then picked up the pace. Verde caressed her breasts and erect nipples and watched with pleasure the sinewy muscles in the soft rise of her belly as she adjusted her hips for maximum penetration. As she was nearing orgasm, she quickened the pace. She was breathing heavily, and Verde could feel her heart racing with both his hands on her breasts. He could see the blissful excitement on her face as she neared her climax. Finally, she took several long thrusts and began quivering and slowed down her pace only after her orgasm ended. Then she picked up the pace again as Verde placed both hands on her backside to assist her motion. When she felt that he was reaching orgasm, she slowed her pace to prolong and extend the duration of his climax.

They both turned on their sides, still intertwined, and felt the quickened heartbeats of each other. After a while, she placed her head on the pillow, facing him. "Well, which is it?"

"What do you mean?"

"You know what I mean. Do you prefer to be on top?"

"Maybe I like it when the woman is on top. Then I can see her nipples becoming erect and her hips moving. Maybe I like to see the expression on her face as she's reaching and then having an orgasm."

"You're being evasive. Everything with you is a maybe."

Verde smiled. "Maybe the next time we'll have to do it sideways and then none of us will be on top."

Rose reached down and gently massaged his manhood until it was fully erect. "And when will that be?"

"Right about…now," he said, smiling.

She lifted one of her legs and wrapped it around his back. Then she reached down and inserted his manhood, and they both moved rhythmically, facing each other for the next ten minutes. Throughout the rest of the night, they had sex in various positions until they fell asleep in a blissful state of exhaustion.

They woke up and had sex standing up in the shower. When they arrived at the Las Vegas police headquarters, they were both tired from the night's activities. Verde could see a noticeable change in her expressions. There was a content, schoolgirl glow about her that she tried unsuccessfully to hide as she put on her businesslike exterior. Verde knew he had broken through her cold exterior and awakened her dormant libido that had long been in hibernation.

Verde and Mancuso took turns with the three-hour interrogation. Dussault gave detailed information of the planning and execution of the heist. He gave all the names of his accomplices. He also stated that Raymond Patriarca sanctioned the robbery. He stated that Remy Gerard, a.k.a. the Frenchman, was the liaison between the robbers and Patriarca. Verde immediately knew that would present a problem. Since the Duce had never talked directly with Patriarca, his testimony would be deemed hearsay and inadmissible as evidence to link Patriarca to the heist. At 1:30 p.m. the interrogation ended. Verde told Stone to take a taxi back to the hotel and pack her bags while he went to the Las Vegas office of the FBI.

An hour later Verde returned to the hotel room. Stone's bags were packed and outside her door. He knocked, and she smiled as she opened the door. "Are we leaving now?"

"We have plenty of time before our flight leaves," Verde said, looking at his wristwatch. "We'll go to the airport, eat a late lunch, and then board our plane."

"How did everything go at the FBI office?"

"Fine. Just about now Colonel Stone is receiving my report on the case."

Stone was mystified, and her smile quickly disappeared. Her face became flush with anger. "You filed your report! Your report! Without any of my input? Then what was that nonsense about how clever *my* plan was? How it was the best piece of police work you've ever been involved in. You credit-grabbing son of a bitch!"

Verde was taken aback. "It's not like that at all. Let me explain."

"It's exactly like that!"

"Calm down, and let me explain."

"Not another word!" she said, wheeling her luggage down the corridor.

"You're making a big mistake."

Stone turned around. "You bet I did. You played me, and I can't believe I fell for it…so convincing…so conniving. I thought I knew you, but you're just too clever for me! And if I ever…ever hear a word about what happen between us last night…I'll lose my badge."

"Rose, this is a misunderstanding. Let…me…explain."

Stone turned and began walking toward the elevator. "Do yourself a favor and don't be on the same flight back. Take a later flight…for your own good." Then she just waved her hand in the air as if to say that she had said enough.

Verde stood in the corridor upset that she wouldn't let him explain the details of what he had filed. At first he did not know how he was going to salvage their relationship. As he began thinking, a wide, devilish smile appeared on his face as he came to realize what was going to happened when she went back to her barracks in the morning. He knew that after tomorrow everything would be rectified, and that she would be his…forever.

***

In the late afternoon, Detective Mancuso escorted Dussault back to Rhode Island, accompanied by a federal sky marshal. Just before they landed at Green Airport, Mancuso stretched, looked at the Duce, and smiled a wide, devious grin.

Dussault noticed Mancuso's smile. "Why do you have that shit-eating grin on your face?"

"Remember the secretary who came into the interrogation room and spilled the file on the desk?"

"Yeah, the one with the nice tits."

"That was Lieutenant Detective Rose Stone of the Rhode Island State Police. She played you like a violin."

"How do you figure that?"

"She's the one who concocted that story about JoJo whacking Floyd and Burns. That story was all bullshit. They're all still alive. You got played."

"Those motherfuckers. And I suppose the plea deal is bullshit also?"

"No, it's real. You'll be placed in protective custody in an undisclosed location until you testify, and then everything you signed in the plea agreement will be fulfilled."

"And suppose I renege of the deal and refuse to testify?"

"Just like Verde said. If you won't testify, you'll be placed in general population in the ACI. How long do you think you'll last in prison with an open contract on your life and a dozen button men just waiting to collect the bounty on your head? Testifying is your only way out."

Dussault sat back in his chair as a stewardess announced their arrival at the airport. He knew Verde and Stone had deceived him. He had underestimated his opponents. He never saw the bluff coming and was beaten at his own game.

***

8:00 a.m., State police headquarters, Scituate, Rhode Island

Detective Stone walked down the long corridor past Colonel Stone's office. The door to his office was partially open, but she didn't believe he saw her walk by. When she entered the cafeteria, a half-dozen state troopers stood up and starting clapping. She was caught off guard, surprised, and confused. Suddenly, the colonel entered the cafeteria and stood behind her. He was an imposing figure and stood nearly a foot taller than her. Stone turned, saw him, and was startled.

"I guess congratulations are in order, Detective Stone," he said in a monotone voice, devoid of all emotion or inflection. He extended his hand to congratulate her. She shook his hand, still puzzled.

"Have you read Agent Verde's report?"

"No, sir, not as of yet."

"Then I guess I'll be the first to congratulate and inform you of the report."

"I don't understand, sir."

"Don't be so modest, Detective Stone. Agent Verde's report and the press release that will be redacted before it's published gives you full credit, along with the assistance of Detective Mancuso, for soliciting Dussault's confession and him signing the plea agreement. We're all proud of your accomplishment, and Attorney General Michaelson called me last night to thank me personally and extend congratulations to you and Mancuso. You will both receive special commendations at our next awards banquet. Once again, congratulations," he said as all of the other troopers in the room clapped. "I have a copy of the report for you in my office. Have you unpacked yet?"

"No, sir."

"Good. You're flying back to Las Vegas in the morning to conduct an interview with Dussault's girlfriend, a Miss Kayla Spelling. We want to trace and document all of Dussault's movements and activities—where they went, how much money he spent, and whom he associated with—when he was in Las Vegas."

"Yes, sir. Will Agent Verde be accompanying me on the trip?"

"I don't believe so. He's going to be busy with procuring arrest warrants and wire taps."

As Rose walked to her office, Sergeant Dunn came strolling down the corridor with a wide grin on his face. "Congratulations, Detective Stone," he said, extending his hand. "I read the report. Looks like you and Mancuso made a fool out of Hollywood."

"Who?"

"Agent Verde."

"I guess we did," she said, with a reluctant half smile.

Rose returned to her office and began reading Verde's report. "I made a fool out of myself," she thought. "He must hate me. I just hope he will forgive me." She was feeling mixed emotions as she read the report. She was elated that he gave credit for the successful conclusion to the investigation, but at the same time she realized she had overreacted when she did not let him explain what he had filed. She finished the report and sat thinking about how she felt like a teenager out on a first date that evening, which ended in a blissful night of sex. She knew she had made a big mistake and wondered how she was going to salvage their relationship. She put down the report and put in a call to his office.

***

Verde's secretary came into his office and told him that there was a call for him from Detective Stone. Verde looked at his wristwatch. "Tell her that I haven't returned from Las Vegas and that I may be in later in the day." She called back several times, and each time Verde's secretary told her he wasn't in. The last time she called, Verde sat back in his chair, placed both hands behind his neck, and smiled.

Omerta

Detective Stone went to Las Vegas to conduct a series of lengthy interviews with Dussault's girlfriend, Kayla. At first she was reluctant to cooperate, but after Stone informed her that if she didn't corporate she could be charged with harboring a fugitive from justice, she revealed every detail of their time spent together, including the intimate details of their sexual arrangement. Over the next few days, Stone, Kayla, and LVPD detectives visited her home, the MGM Hotel, and the various places they shopped and went for gambling and entertainment.

During that time Stone placed many calls into Verde's office. She had not slept well since their altercation and was exasperated over the fact that she couldn't reach him to apologize. On Verde's instructions, she was told that he was on assignment and it was the bureau's policy not to disclose or contact an agent while he was undercover for fear jeopardizing an investigation or compromising an agent's safety. Stone said she understood and that if he did contact the office to tell him that she was in Las Vegas and she would contact him when she returned.

Based upon Dussault's deposition, arrest warrants were issued for all the participants in the Bonded Vault robbery. There was a long-standing adversarial relationship between the Frenchman and Fassbender with detectives Mark and Tom. Verde thought it would be a nice touch, so he was adamant to the Providence police chief that they would be assigned the arrest warrants to pick them up.

Detectives Mark and Tom entered the Peppermint Lounge at lunchtime, knowing that the Frenchman and Fassbender would be there.

When they entered they saw Remy and Jerry sitting with several Providence Public Works Department employees at a large round table in the back room. They were all picking from a large Italian antipasto salad, waiting for their entrées.

"Waiter," Remy said, "another round of drinks." He saw Mark and Tom entering. "Here they are, Providence's finest," he said, with a cocky, arrogant tone as all the men at the table laughed.

Mark walked up behind the Frenchman slowly, leaned over, and began talking with a whisper but loud enough so that all of the other men at the table could hear what he was saying. "Remy, you ever hear of the expression that every dog has its day?"

"Well, douchebag, today's yours!" Tom interjected.

The cocky expression drained from the Frenchman's face as Tom took out his handcuffs and spun them around his finger.

"Today's your day too, Jerry," Mark said. "Looks like you're going to be playing for the ACI all-star softball team for quite some time. I heard they got nice pinstriped uniforms with even your name and number on the back," he said, being facetious.

"What the fuck are you talking about?" Fassbender asked.

"Oh no…I guess you didn't get the memo," Tom said, feigning that they hadn't heard the news. "Your pal Dussault ratted out you and the Frenchman. You're both under arrest for the Bonded Vault robbery.

When the other patrons of the lounge heard what Tom said, the barroom became silent. As Tom handcuffed the Frenchman and Fassbender, Mark read them their Miranda Rights. He added a personal touch while he was reciting them their rights. "You also have the right to remain stupid motherfuckers. You also have the right to resist arrest, which gives me the right to kick the shit out of you scumbags. Did I leave anything out, Mark?"

"No, I think you just about covered it all."

Mark took Fassbender to the ACI intake center to await arraignment in the morning. Verde had instructed them take the Frenchman to the Providence Police holding center. He wanted to talk with him before his arraignment. Before he went to see the Frenchman, Verde met with Attorney General Michaelson and Chief Justice of the Superior Court Joseph Weisberger for an advisory opinion.

Verde shook Attorney General Michaelson's and Chief Justice Weisberger's hands and sat down. Weisberger put down Dussault's deposition and removed his reading glasses. "I've read Dussault's deposition, and I concur with both Verde's and your assessment, Julius. In my opinion, Dussault's testimony would be inadmissible as third-party hearsay and would not lead to an indictment, much less to a conviction, on conspiracy charges for Patriarca's role in the Bonded Vault robbery. However, Remy Gerard would be a material witness that would unequivocally lead to an indictment and conviction for Patriarca on conspiracy charges. Is it your strategy to use a smaller fish to catch the trophy fish, Patriarca?

"Yes, your honor."

It's going to be an uphill battle to coerce Gerard to cooperate and testify, seeing that he is a high-level Mafia associate. As such, he believes and abides by their code of silence, omerta.
Good luck on your fishing expedition, Agent Verde."

"Thank you, your honor," Verde said, getting up to leave. "Julius, I'm going to try to cut a plea deal with the Frenchman for his testimony against Patriarca. I'll let you know how I make out with the Frenchman's interrogation."

***

Later in the afternoon, Verde went to the Providence Police station to interview the Frenchman. He knew Remy Gerard was not your average low-life criminal. He was intelligent, street savvy, and could have easily have been a success at any career he'd chosen if he hadn't taken to a life of crime. He was an avid reader of fiction and nonfiction books on history and military leaders. However, like Verde, he was streetwise long before he became bookwise.

The Frenchman was a high-ranking and well-respected member of the Patriarca crime faction. Verde knew that he adhered to omerta as devoutly as any Christian following the beliefs of his or her religion. Flipping the Frenchman would be a long shot. Conventional tactics would never work on him. Verde decided to use misdirection and play to Remy's vanity, seeing that he considered himself to be an intellectual. Before Verde entered the interrogation, he thought about what Judge Weisberger had said about using a smaller fish to catch a bigger fish. He remembered when his father took him and his brother, along with his uncles and cousins, on a deep-sea fishing charter. He was about twelve years old and asked his father what he was doing when he was baiting his large hook.

"When you want to catch a big fish," Verde's father had said, "you bait your hook with a smaller fish to catch the big one."

With his father's words in mind, Verde entered the small interrogation room. The pale-yellow paint on the walls was peeling, and the room smelled of musty, damp cement. He sat down across from the Frenchman and placed his small brown valise on the table in between them.

His strategy was to play upon the Frenchman's ego, that he considered himself a thinking-man's criminal.

"Remy Gerard," Verde said, looking directly at him. "I knew one day I'd have you in a room just like this one with one of my hands holding a gun to your head and the other squeezing you by the balls."

"Oh no, please, not that," the Frenchman said, feigning that Verde was scaring him, and then he laughed in his face. "First of all, asshole, I never got my phone call, and I demand to have my lawyer present before I answer any questions."

"Be civil now, Remy. Very soon a man a smart as you is going to realize that I can be your guarding angel or the devil of your destruction."

"Who the fuck do you think you're talking to? I'm not the Duce!"

Verde thought back when on that fishing expedition his father had imbedded his hook deeply into a large swordfish and the struggle began. "I thought I'd come to see you before you talked with your attorney. Let's call this an informal conversation, strictly off the record."

The Frenchman rolled his eyes and shook his head from side to side in disbelief to what Verde had just said. "You think I'm a moron. You and I know everything is always on the record."

"On the contrary. I don't think you're a stupid habitual criminal. I know you're a worthy adversary, an intelligent man, a man not to be trifled with. I'm going to show you some pictures and ask you some questions. If you want to answer, fine. If not, you can just listen. That being said, I know that a man as smart as I hope you are will come to the conclusion that I'm the only thing standing between your freedom or spending most of the rest of your life in prison, and maybe saving your life."

"What the fuck are you talking about? Even if I am convicted of conspiracy in the Bonded Vault robbery, and that's still a big 'if,' I'll get what, seven to ten? And I'll be out in four."

Verde remembered when his father was trying to reel in the fish. And it seemed like hours. Sometimes it looked like his father would win the battle, and at other times it looked like his father was tiring and the fish would ultimately go free. "Oh, I think you misunderstood why I'm here," Verde said, with a false look of puzzlement. "You thought I was here *only* to discuss the heist. Well, let me make my intentions clear."

"I don't understand. What did that rat Dussault tell you? What did you have on him that turned this stand-up guy into an informer?"

"I assure you I had much less on him than I have on you. You want to know why he cooperated? I simply made him an offer he couldn't refuse."

The Frenchman laughed. "You've been watching too many *Godfather* movies. Oh, that's right. Didn't I read somewhere that you were a consultant on the first one?"

"Yes, I was, because they wanted authenticity. I know how wise guys walk, talk, and think, and that's why I know you're going to accept my offer."

"Fuck off, Verde. There nothing you can do, say, or promise me that would ever...ever...ever turn me into an informant."

"That's funny," Verde said, pausing and then looking off in the distance as if to recall something. "Those were the exact words the Duce said just before he signed the plea agreement."

"If you're not here to talk about the Bonded Vault robbery, then why the fuck did you come here to see me?"

"A man as smart as you knows you're going to be convicted of the heist, but I'm after a bigger fish. We know the Old Man sanctioned the robbery. We're going to put him away, and you're going to help us do that."

"You want me...me...to help you put the Old Man away! Not in a hundred fucking years!
And besides, you already got the Duce to testify against the Old Man. So why would you need my testimony?"

"Now you must think that *I'm* a moron! You've been through the legal system since you were a teenager. They say you're somewhat of a jailhouse lawyer. You know that the Duce never talked directly with Patriarca. You know that his testimony is inadmissible as hearsay. According to Dussault, you were the liaison between the robbers and the Old Man. That's why we need your testimony, and I'm going to get it."

The Frenchman smiled a sinister grin. "I'll do 'all day' in prison before I become an informant. If you think I'm going to roll on the Old Man, you're pissing up a rope."

"Defiant to the end, is that it? You want to be a good little Mafia soldier with your misguided omerta? Then just sit quietly and listen to my little story."

Verde opened his valise and slid a black-and-white photograph of a small ranch-style house on Golf Avenue, East Providence in front of him. "What can you tell me about this house?"

The Frenchman shrugged his shoulders. "Nothing."

Then Verde placed another photograph in front of him. Isn't that your vehicle in front of that house?" he asked, sliding another photograph in front of him. Before he could answer, he shot out another question. "Isn't that you coming out of that house?"

"Oh yes, now I remember. That's the house that Chucky Floyd rented."

"We've had all the usual suspects under surveillance who could have possibly participated in the Bonded Vault robbery for months." Verde took another photograph of a waterfront bungalow-style house and slid it across the table. "You recognize this house?"

Remy looked at the photograph briefly. "No."

"I don't believe you do. A man as smart as you would have sent his underlings there. It's a mile away as the crow flies from Chucky's house. Do you know this man?" he said, sliding another photograph in front of him.

"No."

"I believe you. A man a smart as you would never have dealt directly with him."

"Who is he?"

"You mean who *was* he? His name was Ralph Imperatore. He had a nice cover as a substitute teacher in Providence. In reality, he was a high-level fence. Here's what I think happened. You can stop me at any time if you think I'm wrong," Verde said, with a touch of sarcasm. "You sent some of your crew to fence part of the valuables from the robbery. Oh yes, at the crime scene, we identified many items taken from Bonded Vault, including canvas bags of bright, uncirculated Morgan silver dollars all dated 1887. Does that ring a bell? The way I figure it, after he gave you about seven hundred grand, you sent your crew back to steal back what you had fenced. They tortured him to find out where he hid the loot. After he bled out and was unconscious, keeping him alive was a moot point. So they chopped him up and went fishing, dumping the body parts in the ocean, using Imperatore's own boat."

"Nice theory, but you and I know you're the one who's fishing."

Verde thought back. His father had regained his second wind and seemed to be winning the battle against the fish. "Oh, I don't think so."

"Where's the evidence?"

"Here's part of it," Verde said, sliding another photograph in front of him. "You know what this is?"

The Frenchman looked at the photograph, but this time he turned it around to study it more carefully. "It's a thumb."

"It's Imperatore's thumb. Your 'cleaning crew' was sloppy. They also left behind fingerprints on the jugs of bleach they used to clean the blood from the crime scene. It's only a matter of time before we tie their fingerprints to the murder, and then they'll cop a plea and rat you out rather than face an M-1 charge, which carries a mandatory life sentence. You'll be charged with conspiracy to commit extortion and conspiracy to commit murder."

Verde watched the facial expressions of the Frenchman. It changed dramatically from one of indifference and defiance to one of genuine concern. As soon as Remy noticed that Verde was observing him, he put on his tough-guy exterior in an attempt to show Verde that what he had said had no effect upon him.

"That's an interesting story, but it's just a weak theory built on circumstantial evidence. But if I did the crime, and that's a big 'if,' I'll do the time. Verde, do you know who you are? You're Machiavelli!"

Verde put the photographs back into his valise and smiled. I never said I was a boy scout. Yes, I am Machiavellian. I'm a deceitful conniving son of a bitch. I'm exactly what I have to be to nail criminals like you. I'll give you a couple days to think over my offer. If you agree to testify against the Old Man, I'll give you immunity from prosecution in the heist, a new identity, a job, and a home in the middle of nowhere. I'll not pursue the M-1 conspiracy and murder charges, and I'm willing to put all that in writing as part of your plea agreement. However, if you won't cooperate by the date of your arraignment, the deal is off the table. I'll recommend to the judge that you serve both sentences concurrently."

"You know as well as I do that I'll run any prison they put me in. I'll have women, booze, and the best of food. It'll be like a country club. And by the way, you'll never, never make the M-1 charges stick."

"Oh, I'll make it stick, and if I don't think the prosecutor can't get a conviction, since you know I'm Machiavelliam, I'll manufacture all the evidence needed to frame you. You'll be an old man when you get out of prison…that is, if you live that long."

Remy laughed. "If I'm in my seventies when I get out," he said, placing his hands behind his head as he leaned back in his chair, "I'll go to Saint Ann's Cemetery. Isn't that the place where all you wops get buried? Then I'll piss on your grave."

Verde got up to leave. He did not want the Frenchman to have had the last word. "After Patriarca hears that we picked you up, he's going to know that only your testimony could send him to prison for the rest of his life. A man as smart as you should be thinking that if the Old Man so easily put out a contract on Dussault, knowing that he could not legally link him to the heist, how long will it be before he has you wacked? You think he's as loyal to you as you apparently are to him? Just thought I'd give you something to think about before your arraignment. As far as Saint Ann's Cemetery is concerned, I have a feeling that's more of a premonition that very soon, if Partiarca has his way, I'll be pissing on your grave!"

Verde closed the door behind him. He remembered his father's excitement when after the long battle he finally saw the swordfish near the bow of the boat, exhausted and ready to give up. One of his uncles was about to use a large hook to bring it aboard when the fish freed itself by breaking the line and swam away. He wondered if that's what would ultimately happen on his fishing expedition with the Frenchman.

Verde Sleeps with the Fishes

Remy Gerard was arraigned on charges for his role in the Bonded Vault robbery. He did not accept Verde's plea agreement. However, Verde had already put a plan into motion in an attempt to tie the Old Man to the heist. A federal judge had signed a court order for wire taps for Patriarca's Coin-O-Matic and on the homes of various known associates of the Old Man. The state-of-the-art bugging devices were almost impossible to detect even using the most sophisticated sweeping devices. The FBI had rented a second-floor apartment a few months earlier across the street from the Old Man's headquarters. Under the guise of Bell Telephone employees, the FBI had set up parabolic microphones on the roof of the building in an attempt to catch *cross talk* about the heist from the Old Man's associates.

Verde's office was overworked and shorthanded. Most of the field agents were working with treasury agents confiscating and tracking the source of massive amounts of nearly perfect counterfeit twenty-dollar bills. The counterfeit bills were being circulated in the New England area with the heaviest concentration in Rhode Island. Verde seldom worked in the field on stakeouts, but because the other agents were working overtime, he took the third shift in rotation as part of the surveillance team across the street from the Old Man's headquarters.

***

6:00 a.m., the following morning

The Providence Police arrived on the scene after an employee of a downtown breakfast restaurant noticed that the guardrail on the banks of the Providence River was smashed and that a car was almost completely submerged with its headlights still on but barely visible through the murky water. The Providence Police ran the back license plate and saw that it was registered to the FBI and issued to Director Vincent J. Verde. It quickly went over the teletype to all local enforcement authorities. They had yet to determine if it was an accident or a crime scene, or if Verde's body was inside the vehicle.

Detective Stone had returned from Las Vegas late the previous night. It was her day off, and she awoke later than usual. She put on her jogging suit and made a cup of coffee. She was just about to go to the health spa for her morning workout when she became horrified as she heard the sketchy details concerning Verde over her police scanner. She quickly changed into her uniform and sped off in an unmarked state police vehicle, lights flashing, toward Providence.

When she arrived several state and Providence police officers had gathered together trying to assess what actually had taken place. A fire truck and rescue vehicle were parked along the guardrail of the Providence River. The area surrounding the scene was sectioned off with yellow caution tape. Local television stations and newspapers had dispatched camera crews and reporters to the scene. Two of the newspaper reporters were taking notes on their yellow legal pads as they asked a state trooper questions. Divers were putting on their wet suits and diving gear and were almost ready to enter the water. A small-crane operator was unrolling a long, thick steel cable with a hook on the end.

Stone immediately sprinted to the guardrail and leaned over, looking at the almost completely submerged vehicle. She knew if he was still in the vehicle, he most certainly was dead. Her mind was racing. Thoughts were flowing through her mind like the rushing water below. His office said he was working undercover. After all, she thought, he was working on a high-profile case involving the Mafia. Did they get to him? Was he getting too close?

A state trooper walked up to her. "Detective Stone, the colonel is on the line. He wants to talk with you."

"I thought this was your day off," Colonel Stone said.

"It is, sir. When I heard that Agent Verde's car was in the Providence River, I came right down."

"Is Agent Verde still in the vehicle? Is he dead?"

"They're about to hoist the vehicle out of the water," she said sadly but calmly, "and then we'll know."

"Call me immediately the minute you know one way or the other."

"Yes, sir."

***

3:00 a.m., earlier that morning

Verde had parked his Crown Victoria behind the apartment complex of the stakeout location. A lone figure stumbled down the deserted dark alleyway off Atwells Avenue. He had been nightclubbing and ended the night drinking at an illegal after-hour's club. It was Rocco Assenzi. He stopped behind Verde's car, unzipped his pants, and pissed on the bumper of the car. Then his eyes opened wide as he recognized the government license plate on the vehicle. He remembered that this was the vehicle that Detective Stone was driving when the EMT's were wheeling him into the rescue squad. He mistakenly believed that it was her vehicle. He reached up and felt the elongated scar on the bridge of his nose, and it was a painful reminder of the altercation with Stone when she broke his nose in two places.

"Payback's a bitch," he mumbled to himself as he quickly scurried to his home several blocks away.

He returned a short while later carrying two lengths of wire with alligator clips on each end, a pair of pliers, and a slim jim burglary device to unlock cars. He opened the lock with the slim jim, and when the alarm sounded, he popped the hood lid and quickly cut the wires on the alarm system. Rocco attached the wires from the solenoid to the starter and battery and started it up. Then he headed toward downtown Providence.

***

7:30 a.m.

Agent Rodrigues ran up the back steps to the apartment that was being used as the stakeout. He used his key and opened the door slowly. Then he drew his revolver and walked into the room. Verde was still asleep. He awoke abruptly and was startled to see Rodrigues standing over him with his gun drawn. Verde's cloths and hair were disheveled. He had a growth of stubble on his face.

"What the fuck's going on?" he asked, still disoriented from having just awakened.

Rodrigues lowered his gun and placed it back in his holster. "I rushed right over when it came over the wire."

"What? What came over the wire?"

"Your Crown Victoria is in the Providence River. Speculation is that you either had an accident or were murdered. Everyone thinks you're dead."

"I've been here all night. Someone must have stolen it. I parked it behind the apartment," he said, getting up and stretching. "We have to get better cots. My back is killing me."

"Come with me. I'll give you a ride downtown."

"Yeah, we better hurry," he said, putting on his wrinkled jacket, "before the newspapers start writing my obituary."

When Verde arrived at the scene, he saw Rose still leaning over the railing, waiting for the crane to lift the vehicle out of the water. As he walked toward her, a state police trooper recognized him and was about to acknowledge his presence. Verde put his finger up to his lips and motioned the trooper to be silent, all the while smiling. He walked up to Stone and stood several feet behind her. Then he cleared his throat. "You think someone's dead down there, officer?"

"I'm sorry, sir," she said, not turning around. "You'll have to stand back."

Verde started laughing. Stone turned quickly, and the look of trepidation disappeared from her face and was replaced by a nervous smile of reassurance and joy. "What happened? You scared the hell out of me."

"Don't get too emotional now," Verde said. "What's this? Is that a tear a see rolling down your cheek?" he asked, smiling.

Stone quickly wiped the tear off her face and tried to regain her composure. "How did your car end up in the Providence River?"

"I don't know. I was on a stakeout and someone must have stolen it."

Stone immediately looked across the street and then called over a state trooper. "You see those buildings across the street, the ones with the surveillance cameras? When those businesses open, ask their security officers for the recordings for last night and take them to our headquarters."

"Yes, Detective Stone," he said.

As she turned her attention back to Verde, she could see he was staring at her. "Don't look at me. I'm a mess. Today's my day off. When I heard your car was in the river, I rushed right over without putting on any makeup or fixing my hair. I must look horrible."

"You look beautiful to me. If today's your day off, maybe you can give me a ride to my apartment. I don't have a ride," he said.

"I have to make a call. The colonel wanted to know if you were all right…or dead. She called Colonel Stone and gave him the details. Then she turned back to Verde. "You know I tried to call you several times when I went to Las Vegas to interview Dussault's girlfriend."

"And what was so urgent that you called my office eleven times?" he asked, with a cunning smile.

"Why you son of a B. You knew I called all those times, and you never returned my call."

"Okay, Rose, what did you want to tell me? Come on; you can say it."

She lowered her head. "I wanted to apologize and tell you that I overacted in Las Vegas. I wanted to thank you for your report on Dussault. I've lost sleep wanting to straighten things out things between us."

"Apology accepted. I too have been dying to get something straight between us," he said, raising his eyebrows, "ever since our night together in Vegas."

Rose thought for a moment and realized the meaning of what he was alluding to and blushed. "Oh, I see."

As they were about to leave, the crane had lifted the vehicle out of the water. Dark, discolored water was pouring out of the vehicle as the crane lowered it onto the pavement. Jim Taricani, a reporter with a local television station, scurried up to Verde. "Agent Verde, was that your vehicle in the river, and how did it get there?"

"Yes, it is, Jim. It was stolen from an undisclosed location last night. But"—he waved his hand in the direction of the water—"the bureau will get to the bottom of this," he said, tongue in cheek. "We always do."

***

Rose entered Verde's apartment and was impressed by how orderly and meticulous it was kept. He had a small office set up next to the living room. On his mahogany rolltop desk were files that were all categorized in alphabetical order and a folder of cases in progress.

Above his desk was a large framed photograph of him from the set of *The Godfather* with various cast members. She looked closely at the signatures of Marlon Brando, Al Pacino, Richard Castellano, and Francis Ford Coppola under their pictures. As Verde took off his weapon and holster and placed it into the desk drawer, Rose picked up a framed award for his role in coordinating the large drug bust against members of the Columbian Cartel. It was dated September 1970 and signed by Clarence Kelly, Director of the FBI.

Verde went into the bathroom to shave and shower. As he was shaving, Rose walked into the bathroom. The quaint bathroom had black and seafoam-green tiles on the walls and gray marble tiles on the floor. He was wearing only a white towel tucked around his waist.

Rose began unbuttoning her blouse. "You won't mind if I take a shower while you shave. In my haste this morning, I didn't take one."

"Certainly," he said, watching her in the mirror as she undressed. "And when I'm done, I'll join you."

Upon entering the shower, Rose handed Verde a bar of soap and turned her back toward him. "Would you wash my back for me, Jay?" she said, handing him a washcloth.

Verde lathered her back. When he was through, he put both arms around her and lathered her breasts, running the bar of soap gently in a circular motion over her nipples. They stayed in that position as the relaxing warm water flowed over them. When he was fully erect, he slid his manhood deeply into her as she lifted her leg slightly to assist him.

After they left the shower, Rose put on one of Verde's white terrycloth bathrobes, which was several sizes too large for her, and wrapped a towel into a turban to dry her damp hair. Verde put on a pair of light blue boxer shorts and a white T-shirt and went into the kitchen to make breakfast. He mixed waffle batter and poured it into a heated Belgian waffle maker. Then he placed some mushrooms, onions, and peppers into a small pan, scrambled up some eggs with a mixture of cream, and poured it over the omelet. Rose sat at the kitchen table and poured two cups of coffee. When the waffles were done, Verde cut up some strawberries and placed them into a bowl in front of Rose. When the omelet was done, he folded each section in half and placed the dish in the middle of the table.

"Just like a married couple," Verde said as Rose rolled her eyes. As she removed the turban and placed it on the chair next to her, she noticed that Verde was in a trance, staring at her.

"What are you thinking about now?"

"I was wondering what you must have been thinking when you thought I was dead."

Stone became introspective. "I was thinking…" she said, pausing as she thought about something clever to say. Then she looked across the room at the framed photograph from *The Godfather*. "I was thinking that maybe you were sleeping with the fishes." She joked with him.

Verde looked over his shoulder and saw the photograph she was looking at. "Clever girl."

As Rose leaned forward to put some strawberries on her waffle, the front of her bathrobe came undone, exposing one of her breasts. "I was thinking that I'd never see you again, that I'd never get a chance to tell you so many things I wanted to say."

Verde cut the omelet and placed half in front of Rose. He sat down across from her. She took a small bite and smiled. "You're a good cook."

"This is just a simple breakfast. My mother wanted daughters, and she had two boys. She taught us how to cook all her favorite Italian dishes. Some night I'll have you over and I'll make my signature dish, veal saltimbocca."

"I'd like that," she said, placing some strawberries on her waffles.

"You really didn't answer my question," Verde said, staring at Rose. "I want to know what you were really thinking when I saw you leaning over the railing. Were you thinking that maybe I was dead? Maybe you were thinking that your last chance for happiness and a family, the man you were falling in love with, was at the bottom of the river."

Rose choked on a piece of the waffle she had in her mouth. She cleared her throat. "Wishful thinking."

"Not for me."

Rose realized that he was being serious. "What do you mean by that?"

"You must have sensed that I've always been attracted to you, even though I knew you despised me."

"I wouldn't say that."

"You didn't have to. It was obvious. I know you hated me ever since I got all the credit for that big drug bust even though you did a fair amount of the investigative work, and you thought that's what was going to happen again in the Bonded Vault case."

"Maybe my opinion of you evolved, changed." Rose noticed that Verde was lost in a trance again. "What? What are you thinking about now?"

"I was thinking how beautiful, sexy, and smart you are. How compatible we are. We're not getting any younger, you know."

"What's that suppose to mean?"

"What I'm saying is that I love everything about you."

"About me?"

"I guess what I'm saying is that I love you."

Rose was dumbfounded. His declaration of love had caught her off guard. "You love me?" she asked, in a voice slightly above a whisper.

"Yes, I do. How do you feel about that? Here's what I propose. I think we should date for a while and see what develops. Yes, we're both strong willed, and we'll have our disagreements, as any couple does, but I know we're compatible. We have similar interests and careers. Maybe in time if you feel the same way as I do, we could get married."

Rose looked at Verde and became pensive. "I don't know what to say. This is unexpected. Is this a marriage proposal?"

"You want me to get down on one knee?" Verde said jokingly. "Yes, yes this is a marriage proposal."

"All right, we'll give it some time and see what develops, but I'm not accepting or promising you anything...yet."

Verde got up and filled her cup with coffee. Before he could sit down, Rose stood up, opened her bathrobe, put her arms around him, and gave him a kiss. Then she took his manhood from the opening in his boxer shorts and massaged it until it was fully erect. "Now let's see if you can get something straight between us…once again."

***

A week later, based on the surveillance tapes from the buildings across the street from the Providence River, an arrest warrant was issued for Rocco Assenzi. He was charged and convicted of stealing government property, destruction of government and city property, and malicious mischief. He was remanded to the Adult Correction Institution, where he received a three-year sentence and was ordered to pay restitution.

The Show Must Go On

All the defendants who participated in the Bonded Vault robbery were apprehended and arraigned except for Mitch "Lucky" Lanogue and Bobby "Big Mac" Macari, who went into hiding and were still at large. Before the trial, JoJo Dancer signed a plea agreement in exchange for his testimony against the other defendants.

As the trial was about to begin, the jury was sequestered at the downtown Providence Holiday Inn Hotel. Judge Anthony Giannini instructed the jury not to watch television accounts or read the newspaper articles relating to the trials.

Judge Giannini had all the defendant's lawyers and the state prosecutors attend a pretrial meeting. He read them the "riot act" and in concise language gave them a stern warning. He told them that this would be a high-profile case covered by many television stations and newspapers throughout the country. He would not allow any "showboating or grandstanding" and would throw any attorney out of his courtroom if they violated his order. He told them that this was going to be a long, exhausting series of trials, and he would keep it "tight" and "civil" or else.

At the pretrial hearing, he instructed all the attorneys and state prosecutors that he didn't want the jury distracted by the inferences to New England crime boss, Raymond Patriarca. He said although Dussault told the grand jury that the Old Man, the numero uno, a.k.a. Raymond Patriarca, had sanctioned the robbery, his testimony would be regarded as hearsay and he would not allow the use of that reference to cloud the main issues of each defendant's trial.

***

On August 2, 1975, almost a year after the heist, the first series of trials began. Metal detectors were installed at the entrance of the downtown courthouse. No cameras or recording devices were allowed into the courtroom. Newspapers hired artists to sketch likenesses of the judge, the defendants, their lawyers, and state prosecutors to accompany articles in their newspapers.

Between the cameramen, newspaper and television reporters, and the hundreds of spectators outside the courtroom, the excitement and suspense surrounding the trials was palpable. One out-of-state newspaper reporter's article stated that they "did everything but sell popcorn outside the carnival atmosphere of the courthouse."

Verde attended the trial on a regular basis, and when Stone came, they sat together. At other times, Stone came accompanied by several state police detectives and sat with them.

Every day that Dussault would testify, he was transported from an undisclosed location by a caravan of sheriffs and state police through electronic gates to a secured bunker under the courthouse. Once inside, he was escorted to a secure anteroom next to the courtroom by sheriffs carrying shotguns and automatic weapons.

Due to the series of articles by television and newspaper reporter Jack White, the public learned the details of how Detective Mancuso and Detective Rose Stone, assisted by the FBI, coerced Dussault with a false narrative into becoming a witness for the prosecution. Even though Dussault knew he had been duped into becoming an informant, he was going to testify. At this point, his only choice was to let the show go on.

Baby, although I chose

This lonely life,

It seems it's strangling

Me now.

All those wild men,

Big cigars,

Gigantic cars,

They're all laughing at the lie.

Oh, I've been used,

I've been a fool

Oh, what a fool,

I broke all the rules,

But I must let the show go on.

—Three Dog Night, "The Show Must Go On"

The ringmaster in the center stage of the three-ring circus was Robert Dussault. He played his role in the persona as mobster "The Duce," and his performance would not fail to delight and entertain his audience. Every time he took the witness stand, he had a cocky *wise-guy* smirk on his face and walked with a defiant swagger. One newspaper reporter wrote that "Dussault talked the talk and walked the walk of a lifelong gangster." He lived up to his star billing and became a *media darling* as they ate up all his antics. He joked and talked with the language and dialect of a gangster as he gave his testimony in intimate and graphic details about the planning and execution of the heist. At times Judge Giannini had to admonish him for his vulgar terminology and outlandish levity. The courtroom became silent, and his eyes seemed to well up with tears as he told how his lifelong friend,

Chucky Floyd, was sent to Las Vegas to whack him in an attempt to silence him, believing that he was about to become an informant.

At other times, his testimony was defiant, expressing rage with "the bravado of Sonny Corleone from the movie *The Godfather*," as one reporter wrote in his depiction of Dussault's demeanor in the courtroom. "It was like watching a mob movie," the reporter went on to say, "only better, because this was real life, and destined to be put on the big screen."

As the weeks of testimony went on, Dussault did not come off as a vicious criminal, and the public as well as the media seemed to romanticize his role in the robbery.

Upon cross examination, all the defendant's lawyers pointed out to the jury the details of the generous plea agreement in exchange for, as one lawyer kept emphasizing, a "rat" that was a puppet for the prosecution. Remy Gerard's lawyer went one step further and asked Dussault if his relationship with the state was an "unholy alliance" that gave him an incentive to falsely implicate his client in exchange for the "generous rewards" he would receive for his testimony. However, even though every defense attorney tried to discredit his testimony, Dussault did not waiver from his story and appeared to be a truthful and creditable witness.

As the trials proceeded into the second month, the circulation of the local newspaper, the *Providence Journal*, quadrupled. As one traveled down the mean streets of Atwells Avenue each morning, one could see everyone reading the accounts of the previous day's court activities, on the sidewalks of outdoor cafes and bistros. Local bookies were laying odds and taking bets on the conviction or acquittal of each defendant on trial.

Three Little Words

As the trial was entering the third month, Verde and Stone coordinated their vacation time. He booked an ocean-front suite for a week at the Manchebo Hotel on the Dutch Caribbean Island of Aruba.

They arrived late in the afternoon at sunset. As they left the airport, they felt the warm constant winds blowing across the small seventeen-mile-long island. All of the indigenous divi-divi trees outside their hotel were twisted and pointed in the same direction, shaped by the prevailing winds. As they walked to their room, small brightly colored tiny lizards and geckos dashed across the walkways and quickly disappeared in between the colorful exotic fauna surrounding the hotel. Overhead were coconut, papaya, and mango trees, with their fronds swaying in the wind.

After unpacking they decided to eat a late dinner. All the five-star restaurants on the island required formal dress attire. Verde wore a dark-blue pinstriped suit, and Stone wore a sheer light-orange cocktail dress. They went to a restaurant specializing in French cuisine. After dinner, they took off their shoes and walked along the shore, holding hands like high school sweethearts, back to their hotel. They took a late-night swim in the Olympic-size pool, had a few tropical drinks at the outdoor bar, and returned to their room for an evening of sex.

Having exhausted themselves from the previous night's activities, they slept until noon time. After brunch, they went to the hotel's beach. The Manchebo Hotel was renowned for having the best beach on the island. Tall coconut and date palm trees dotted the beach, which featured sand so white and fine it resembled and had the consistency of sugar. There were many huts scattered over the long stretch of beach. The thatched rooftops of the cabanas were made from interwoven dried palm fronds. At various locations scattered across the beach were small bars in huts serving tropical drinks. They took a swim in the warm, shimmering aqua-blue water and then rested in their partially shaded hut. Verde bought two piña coladas, and they sipped the drinks falling asleep, still tired from the evening before.

A short while later, Verde awoke to the sound of laughter and the talking of a dozen young Swedish men and women in their twenties. They were interns on the island, serving the hotel and restaurant industry. They unpacked their attire in a hut next to an area set up with a volleyball net. Much to Verde's amazement and delight, they all began removing their bathing suits. Then they liberally applied each other with suntan lotion and began playing volleyball. Verde looked over at Rose, who was still sleeping, and tipped up his sunglasses to get a better look at the activities. Rose awoke abruptly as a volleyball came whizzing overhead. Verde stood up and picked up the ball. A very tall blond woman came running over and smiled as he handed it back to her.

Rose slid up her sunglasses, looked at the naked woman, took a sip from her drink, and gave Verde an odd look. "What's going on here?"

"I guess nudity on the beach is a custom on these islands," he said, with a sheepish grin.

"Were you enjoying yourself while I was sleeping? Maybe we should go to another beach."

Verde laughed. "My, my, my, what a prude. Oh, now I see. Rose, are you jealous?"

"Hardly," she said as she looked over at some of the men whose private parts were bouncing about as they played.

Suddenly, Verde made a gesture, pointing to him and Rose. Then he stood up and appeared to be untying his bathing trunks. "Come on, honey; take off your bathing suit. I think they want us to play with them."

"Are you crazy? I'm not taking off my bathing suit in public!"

As she looked at the men and women playing volleyball, she did not notice any of them looking in their direction. When she looked back at Verde, he had a childish grin on his face. Rose realized that he had been toying with her.

"Always playing someone, trying to rent space in someone's head. We should go to a more private beach."

"It was a *joke*. I was just *joking*. And besides, the brochure said this is the best beach on the island, and the scenery is so…stimulating."

"After last night I don't think you need any more stimulation, and besides, I should be more than enough stimulation for you. If you really want to stay, we'll stay."

"Then we'll stay, but if you really want to go, we'll go. You don't have anything to be jealous about, even if all the *tall* blond women are built like *Playboy* centerfolds," he said, tipping up his sunglasses to get another look.

Stone rolled her eyes and gave him a soft whack on his arm. "I'm not jealous."

"I know you're not. And you know why I know you're not jealous?"

"No, enlighten me?"

"Because you know that I know that I'm with the most beautiful and sexy woman on the entire island."

Rose leaned back on her lounge chair, took a sip from her drink, and gave Verde a false smile. "It's too late to butter me up."

Verde turned sideways on his lounge chair, facing Rose. "Look at me," he said. Rose slid up her sunglasses and sat up on her lounge chair. Verde paused. She could tell he was searching, grasping for the right words. Then he began speaking with a solemn tone and a solemn expression on his face. "I've been looking for a woman just like you all my life. As time went by, I didn't think I'd ever find a woman like you. Now I know there's no one in this world for me…except you."

Rose didn't know how to respond. She could see that he was being sincere and that his words were coming from his heart. It was at that exact moment, she would tell him years later, that she decided that after she passed the bar examination, she would accept his marriage proposal. "Okay, you're forgiven," she said, flipping down her sunglasses and lying back on the lounge chair. Then, when she was sure he wasn't looking, a wide smile appeared on her face.

"I'm still waiting for those three little words, darling," Verde said. "Come on; you can say it."

Rose knew what he wanted her to say. In light of him teasing her with the nude sunbathers, she thought she'd give him back some of his own medicine. "And are those three little words 'Go fuck yourself?'"

"Rose, how out of character!" Verde said, genuinely astonished.

"It was a *joke*. I was *joking*," she said, mocking him. "What's the matter, Mr. Verde? You can give it, but you can't take it? Lighten up. I know you wanted me to tell you that I love you, and as I said, I'm not ready to make that commitment, *darling*," she said with a coy, smug smile, nodding to herself, as she believed she had just bested him at his own game.

The Verdict

When Jay and Rose arrived back in Rhode Island, the September climate was a sharp contrast to their vacation paradise. The air was crisp, and it had been raining for nearly a week. The leaves were changing from dark green to brilliant hues of yellow, orange, and red. It had been almost three months since the largest and most expensive trial in Rhode Island's history began. The jury had been in deliberations for over a week, and an announcement was made that they had reached multiple verdicts for all defendants.

The largest crowd to date assembled outside the courthouse to await the results. The media had set up camera crews, and reporters were rehearsing sound bites in preparation for the announcement of the verdicts.

One at a time, the defendants were escorted into the courtroom. Remy Gerard, Chucky Floyd, and Skippy Burns were convicted for their roles in the heist. After capture, Mitch "Lucky" Lanogue and Bobby "Big Mac" Macari had pleaded "no contest" and were convicted as well. Because of conflicting and insufficient evidence, Jerry Fassbender and Jake "The Snake" Tarzanian were acquitted.

After Fassbender was acquitted, he delivered a lengthy diatribe before the court about how the attorney general and state prosecutors had tried to manufacture evidence in an attempt to tie him to robbery and frame him. He thanked the jury, as he put it, for "seeing through the lies." A week later at the sentencing hearing, all the defendants who were convicted received lengthy prison sentences.

Two weeks later, Verde went to the "safe house" at Fort Devens in Massachusetts, where Dussault had been kept under military guard. He was scheduled to be transferred to his new home in the Midwest. Dussault had been given a new social security number along with a new identity under the name Robert Dempsey.

There was an armed military guard posted outside Dussault's room. He was packing the new wardrobe the government had purchased for him. He did not know Verde was coming to see him and was startled and surprised when he entered the room.

"Agent Verde," the Duce said, with a cocky grin. "I don't know if I should shake your hand or tell you you're a fucking asshole," he said, holding up his middle finger.

"Well Mr. Dempsey—that is your new name, is it not?—let's put this into prospective. Would you rather be spending years in prison with the Frenchman, Floyd, and Burns?"

"I was only busting your balls," he said, extending his hand and then shaking Verde's. "I guess this was the best way out, the only way out. It would only have been a matter of time before the Old Man paid some prison guards big money to set me up and have one of his lackeys shank me."

"You're not out of the woods yet. You'll have to keep a low profile, and behave. Remember the mob will only be able to find you if you blow your cover. And believe me, if you fuck up, we'll be there watching you. You won't see us. You won't even know you're under surveillance, but we'll be around. The question is, do you think you can lead a straight life?"

"Me?" he said, grinning. "No fuckin' way! Well, maybe for a while. Can you picture me leading a nine-to-five bullshit existence? I can't promise you that."

"That's the price you'll have to pay for your freedom...and your life. I don't want to have to be chasing you all over the country again, or find that you blew your cover and the mob cut you up into small pieces to make an example out of you."

"You read my jacket, Verde. I've been living the lifestyle of a wise guy, pulling down scores all my life. And now you want me to put on a show, like I did in the courtroom. You want me masquerade as Mr. Joe Citizen."

Verde stood up to leave. "The only advice I can give you is this. Don't squander the new life you have been given. Very few ever receive a second chance." Verde stood up and shook Dussault's hand. "Good-bye, Mr. Dempsey, and good luck. I hope I never see you again."

> Baby, I wish you'd
> Help me escape,
> Help me get away.
> Leave me outside my (new) address
> Far away from this
> Masquerade.
> Cause I've been blind
> Oh, so blind.
> I wasted time
> Wasted, wasted, wasted time.
> Walking on the wire
> High wire

But I must let the show go on.

—Three Dog Night, "The Show Must Go On"

Legacy

Six months after the Bonded Vault trial ended, Rose graduated from Suffolk Law School and passed the Rhode Island bar examination. Shortly thereafter Verde and Stone were married in a small, private ceremony with only close relatives and select members of the state police and the FBI in attendance. They purchased a custom Tutor-style home overlooking the Jamestown Bridge in southern Rhode Island.

Within several years they had two children, a boy that they named Raymond and a girl named Angelica. A decade later, Rose Verde retired from the state police and took a position as a prosecutor with the Rhode Island attorney general's office.

After many years with the FBI, Jay had one week left before he retired. On his last week, he attempted to tie up all loose ends by reviewing all his cold cases in preparation to transfer the files to the new director of the Rhode Island Organized Crime Task Force. As he went through his files, he regretted never having solved the torture and murder of Ralph Impertore. He knew that his murder was linked to the Bonded Vault robbery, but informants and subsequent investigations never developed any solid leads in the case.

Just about the time he was to retire, the Old Man, Raymond Patriarca, died peaceably in his small raised ranch in Johnston, Rhode Island. Everyone knew he sanctioned the Bonded Vault robbery, but he was never brought to trial for his role in the heist. In keeping with the Old Man's wishes, he never did serve another day in prison since his release in 1974. He was buried with all the pomp and circumstance befitting a Mafia don, in a gray granite mausoleum in the Gates of Heaven Cemetery in Barrington, Rhode Island.

In the same time period of Patriarca's death, there was a development in one of Verde's cold cases. One of Frank "BoBo" Marrapese's mob associates was arrested on an intent-to-deliver charge, involving a large quantity of drugs. In exchange for a plea agreement, he turned state's evidence and testified in graphic detail how BoBo had executed Richard "Dickie" Callei and how they disposed of the body in a shallow grave. Based upon his testimony, Marrapese was convicted and received a life sentence nearly ten years after the execution.

Jerry Fassbender, who was acquitted in the Bonded Vault robbery, eventually ran afoul of the law on a first-degree murder charge. He and his brother were tried and convicted for the murder of a mob associate and close friend. It was alleged that Fassbender was ordered to execute loan shark and enforcer George Basmajian after he was bragging that he and Fassbender were sent to whack a mobster who was a suspected informant and threw him off of a twenty-story balcony in New York. In court it was alleged that Fassbender was ordered to execute Basmajian because the mob echelon believed he had violated the mob oath of omerta, and eventually it would implicate them.

As Verde reviewed his files, he took a trip down memory lane of some of the cases and criminals he had been involved with in his long career. He came across the file of Rocco Assenzi. He remembered vividly when his wife had given him an "attitude adjustment," as it was described in the file, and broke his nose in two places after he attempted to assault her. After serving time for dumping Verde's car in the Providence River, Rocco spent the better part of the next decade in prison on various charges.

Rocco died at the young age of fifty-one. His family said he died from a heart attack. However, the coroner's report stated that the cause of death was from a drug overdose, "from a speedball," a deadly combination of heroin and cocaine.

After retiring, Verde was offered the position of chief of police in a small south county community in Rhode Island. Before accepting the position, he was asked to be a consultant on a mob movie shot on location in nearby Massachusetts. The movie, *The Departed*, was directed by Martin Scorsese and revolved around the criminal activities of a Whitey Bulger–type character played by Jack Nicholson. The all-star cast featured Leonardo DiCaprio, Matt Damon, and Martin Sheen.

In 1977, Governor J. Joseph Garrahy nominated Rose Stone for the judicial position as Special Master of the Superior Court. She was confirmed by an overwhelming majority by the Rhode Island Legislature. Over twenty years after the Bonded Vault robbery, their daughter received her law degree and worked in the consumer's fraud division at the Rhode Island attorney general's office.

Remy Gerard, a.k.a. The Frenchman, was serving a life sentence in a North Carolina prison for violating the "three strikes" mandate. He wrote a book detailing his life in the underworld entitled, *What Price Providence*. He knew that the revelations in his book violated omerta. About the time he wrote the book, he had been diagnosed with terminal cancer. Knowing that his life was nearing its end, maybe he wanted to "set the record straight" and ensure his legacy in the history of Rhode Island's mob lore. Needless to say, the book did not go over too well with the dwindling members of Rhode Island's underworld. He died at the age of seventy-five shortly after the book was published.

***

This spring day was a special occasion for the Verde family. Their son had followed in his parent's footsteps and was graduating from the State Police Training Academy. The leaves on the trees were just emerging in various colors. As the crowd gathered, Jay reflected on the long journey that had led him and his family to this day. Rose, as a proud mother, suppressed her tears of joy as she saw her son take the stage with the other candidates. Standing next to Jay was his brother. He straightened out his life and had not been in prison for over a decade. He now had a high-paying job with Local 57, erecting skyscrapers all over the East Coast. He had a stable life and reconciled with his estranged wife. His two boys had inherited his athletic ability and were all-state baseball pitchers in a private school. They had already been offered scholarships to play baseball in college. Ray told his brother he was pleased that his sons would use the talent God had given them and not squander their ability as he once did.

As the ceremony began, Jay looked at his wife and smiled as he thought how fortunate he was to have such a beautiful and accomplished wife who loved him. He gave her a discrete pat on her backside. Rose looked at him, raised her eyebrows, and placed his hand back in front of him. Suddenly, she noticed that an attractive but overweight woman wearing a long black dress and dark sunglasses kept looking back in their direction.

Rose nudged her husband once again. "Someone is scoping you out," she said, with a false smile. "A member of your fan club, I would presume?"

"Where?" Jay asked, not knowing what she was alluding to. He looked in the direction his wife had nodded her head but didn't recognize anyone.

***

As the parade of dignitaries and politicians delivered their long-winded speeches, his thoughts digressed. It had been years earlier. Even though he had been long retired from the FBI, his name was still attached as the case officer in charge of the Dussault/Dempsey file. He had received a notice that Robert Dempsey, a.k.a. Robert "The Duce" Dussault, had died from an apparent heart attack. Even though he was retired, he felt obligated to close out the witness protection file on Dussault. Along with the death notice, he was updated on Dussault's activities since he entered the witness protection program. Dussault had been arrested and imprisoned twice for bank robberies in Colorado and for receiving and selling stolen goods in North Dakota.

Jay traveled to the Thompson/Larson Funeral home in North Dakota. That funeral home was the designated place of internment for anyone in the federal witness protection program in that region. After a small videotaped ceremony with only the funeral director, Jay, and two workers present, they opened the coffin. Even though Dussault looked much older and frail, a mere shadow of the cocky gangster once known as "The Duce," Jay nodded his head when the funeral director asked him on tape if this was Robert Dussault. Then one of the workers closed the casket and lowered it into the ground.

Rose looked over to her husband and noticed that his thoughts were elsewhere. Their son's name was about to be called, and she gave him a slight elbow to his side, which brought him back to the moment. His daughter had taken up a place near the stage to take pictures of her brother as he received his diploma.

After his son received his diploma and the formal ceremony ended, a woman was taking a photograph of his son with a female state police graduate. The female graduate was tall, well built, and attractive. Her hair was neatly pushed back under her graduation cap. Jay and his wife walked over to the young female recruit and his son. She reminded him of another attractive woman he knew from a distant time and place.

The woman who had been taking their photograph was the same one that Rose said had been scoping him out earlier.

"Jay," the woman said. "Jay Verde. I knew it was you."

Verde didn't seem to recognize her. She smiled and took off her dark sunglasses. "It's me, Jennifer Del Marco, from the old neighborhood. I'm married now. My last name is now Trainor. My husband is around here somewhere."

Rose secretly acknowledged the woman to herself, remembering the stories Jay had told her about Jennifer. "Jennifer, this is my wife, Rose," Verde said.

"I know who you are," Jennifer said. "Over the years I've followed both of your careers. Jay and I grew up together. All the girls up the Hill had a crush on your husband and his brother, but Jay was always so quiet and reserved."

"Oh, I bet they all did," Rose said, nodding her head and winking at her husband. "Pleased to finally meet you," Rose said. "Over the years I've heard so much about you."

"What a coincidence. Our lives have come full circle, and now my daughter any your son will be working together. Don't you think they make a fine couple?"

Rose raised her eyebrows, and Jay smiled and nodded with a resounding yes.

Jennifer's husband was calling her over to take a photograph with the lieutenant governor. "I gotta go, Jay, but I'm sure we'll be seeing each other again. Nice to meet you, Rose," she said, scurrying away.

Jay and Rose sat back down in the stands while their son mingled with some of his classmates. As he held Rose's hand, his mind digressed once again. He remembered when he had interviewed Dussault in Las Vegas when the Duce said that they would both die alone with no one to morn their passing. For Dussault half of his prediction came true. He did die alone and lonely with no one to morn his passing, in the middle of a cold, desolate place in North Dakota. That wasn't to be his fate, Jay thought. He had a beautiful and loving wife and two talented children who would carry on both his and his wife's legacies.

Jay thought how fate had brought together the Bonded Vault robbery, his wife, and him. He saw all the characters in that segment of his life vividly, as if it had happened yesterday—Dussault, Kayla, the Frenchman, the Old Man, Freddie the Kook, Rocco Assenzi, Detectives Mark and Tom, and all the other participants in the Bonded Vault robbery and investigation. They were now all intertwined and inseparable from him and his wife's destiny and past, and forever engrained in his memory. It all came together in August 1975. That was the day eight brazen criminals pulled off the heist of a secret mob vault that would forever be known in the annals of Rhode Island's infamous history as the Bonded Vault robbery.

27077637R00108

Made in the USA
Columbia, SC
22 September 2018